T0358359

Cambridge Elements ≡

Elements in Histories of Emotions and the Senses
edited by
Rob Boddice
Tampere University
Piroska Nagy
Université du Québec à Montréal (UQAM)
Mark Smith
University of South Carolina

ZIONISM

Emotions, Language and Experience

Ofer Idels
Ludwig Maximilian University of Munich

CAMBRIDGE
UNIVERSITY PRESS

Shaftesbury Road, Cambridge CB2 8EA, United Kingdom

One Liberty Plaza, 20th Floor, New York, NY 10006, USA

477 Williamstown Road, Port Melbourne, VIC 3207, Australia

314–321, 3rd Floor, Plot 3, Splendor Forum, Jasola District Centre,
New Delhi – 110025, India

103 Penang Road, #05–06/07, Visioncrest Commercial, Singapore 238467

Cambridge University Press is part of Cambridge University Press & Assessment,
a department of the University of Cambridge.

We share the University's mission to contribute to society through the pursuit of
education, learning and research at the highest international levels of excellence.

www.cambridge.org
Information on this title: www.cambridge.org/9781009517423

DOI: 10.1017/9781009442947

First published 2024

A catalogue record for this publication is available from the British Library.

ISBN 978-1-009-51742-3 Hardback
ISBN 978-1-009-44292-3 Paperback
ISSN 2632-1068 (online)
ISSN 2632-105X (print)

Cambridge University Press & Assessment has no responsibility for the persistence
or accuracy of URLs for external or third-party internet websites referred to in this
publication and does not guarantee that any content on such websites is, or will
remain, accurate or appropriate.

Zionism

Emotions, Language and Experience

Elements in Histories of Emotions and the Senses

DOI: 10.1017/9781009442947
First published online: December 2024

Ofer Idels
Ludwig Maximilian University of Munich

Author for correspondence: Ofer Idels, Oferidels@gmail.com

Abstract: Is the history of emotions a methodology or a subject? What is the relationship between emotions and culture? What role does the body play in the human experience? Addressing these questions and more, this element emphasizes the often-overlooked role of emotional and sensory experiences when examining the Zionist experience in the early twentieth century. Focusing on the visceral and embodied historical aspects of the linguistic modernization of Hebrew, it argues that recent cultural studies on Jewish daily life in Palestine have reached an impasse, which the history of emotions could help us overcome. Interpreting Zionist texts not solely as symbolic myths but as a historical, lived experience, this element advocates for the significance of the history of emotions and experience as an innovative methodology with profound ethical implications for our polarized era.

Keywords: Zionism, Hebrew culture, history of emotions, history of experience, Ethics

ISBNs: 9781009517423 (HB), 9781009442923 (PB), 9781009442947 (OC)
ISSNs: 2632-1068 (online), 2632-105X (print)

Contents

1 Introduction   1

2 Experience: Emotions, Culture, and the History
  of Zionism   6

3 Hebrew Revival: Cultural History and the Experience
  of Language   16

4 Eating the Grain: Reading Sources, Ethics,
  and Receptiveness   32

5 A Brief Epilogue on the Emotions of Past and Present   39

References   43

1 Introduction

What is Zionism? Existing scholarship, encompassing intellectual, political, social, and cultural perspectives, has portrayed modern Jewish life in early twentieth-century Palestine as both nationalistic and colonial, original and derivative, radical and bourgeois, empowering and oppressive. Amidst these diverse and sometimes conflicting viewpoints, much of the extensive literature is rooted in theories and ideas that are several decades old, often providing limited explanatory power. Departing from these established perspectives, this study ventures into new directions by exploring questions and insights emerging from twenty-first-century methodologies, which have largely been overlooked by scholars of Zionism: the histories of emotions, senses, and lived experiences.

The apparent scarcity of literature on the Hebrew experience is somewhat surprising, given the pivotal role emotions and the senses played in the Zionist Revolution and modern Jewish existence in Palestine and Israel. We can even boldly posit that, beyond the pursuit of statehood, territorial control, or cultural creation, the paramount goal, achievement, and legacy of Zionism is the formation of a distinct Jewish experience. While this acknowledgment serves as a central theme of this study, the emphasis primarily lies on historiographical rather than historical discussion. Consequently, it provides a methodological and theoretical reflection that may captivate the interest of scholars in both Zionism and Jewish studies, on one hand, and historians of emotions, senses, and experiences, on the other.

This is not a straightforward task, as at this point in time, engaging in the historical exploration of emotions, senses, and experiences still presents a fundamental challenge of definition. For instance, historians of emotions, as outlined by Katie Barclay, approach (and understand) their emerging subfield in at least three distinct ways (Barclay, 2020: 9–12). Other experts might propose different division, as the diversity of the field reflects not only its current popularity but also the lack of a clear agreement on what emotions are and how to study them. These are significant questions, and, without satisfactory answers, the discipline may soon seek alternative and novel approaches to "doing history."

In the pursuit of definition and terminology, this study aligns with the contemporary effort to integrate the sub-fields of emotions, senses, under the banner of "experience" (Boddice & Smith, 2020). By emphasizing the intersections between emotions and the senses, I specifically focus and ponder on three central and interrelated theoretical dilemmas: the role of the body in shaping meaning and experience, the relationship between emotions and culture, and finally, whether the history of emotions should be considered a subject or a methodology. Ultimately, advocating for a perspective that highlights the primary significance of the history of experience is its methodological potential to address some of the contemporary limitations of cultural history.

Section 2 establishes this interpretation of the history of experience and explains why it is essential for the historiography of Zionism. This hypothesis is further tested in the third section, which is dedicated to a historical and historiographical analysis of experience and language through the prism of Hebrew Revival. The fourth section highlights the methodological and ethical opportunities inherent in the history of experience.

Navigating these issues requires delicacy, influenced not only by the current methodological state of the history of emotions and the senses but also by the sensitive political nature of the second pillar of this text – Zionism. It is no secret that in our current moment, discussing Zionism may be nearly impossible without encountering controversy. Even a seemingly straightforward claim, such as stating that Zionism is primarily a national movement, may quickly face criticism from proponents of settler colonialism theories, while, for others, merely suggesting a connection between Zionism and colonialism will be considered a form of blasphemy. This passionate advocacy or dissent, as noted by Derek Penslar (Penslar, 2023), is itself a reflection of the fundamental emotional aspect that has characterized Zionism from its inception. Yet, given these circumstances, it might seem somewhat futile to argue that the following discussion will transcend the polemics with facts and logic. After all, as Hayden White taught us, any historical narrative is inherently political (White, 1973). With that in mind, I acknowledge the politicized nature of the subject matter and, rather than avoiding it, embrace the challenge of providing an intellectual engagement that will, hopefully, encourage Zionists, Anti-Zionists, and anyone else who reads this text, to contemplate the convolutions of both the past and the present.

Once this premise is addressed, a concise historical overview of Zionism becomes necessary. Largely stemming from the disillusionment of European Jews with the unfulfilled promises of assimilation during the Jewish enlightenment (*Haskalah*) and the escalating wave of pogroms and antisemitism, Zionism was just one of the many responses within the diverse landscape of Jewish thought at the turn of the century and in early twentieth-century Europe. Thus, alongside Bundism, Territorialism, Yiddishism, and various other Jewish movements and ideas, it engaged in constant debates – and sometimes negotiations – concerning the future of the Jewish people amidst the challenges of modernity (Frankel, 1984; Bartal, 2005; Moss, 2021).

Throughout this transformative era of High Colonialism, marked by the mass immigration of both European Jews and non-Jews to the "New World," Zionists – referring to Zion, one of the names of Jerusalem – stood out by emphasizing Palestine, or the Land of Israel (*Eretz Yisrael*), as the ultimate solution to the challenges of modern Jewish life. Nevertheless, even within Zionism there was a lack of homogeneity, as it encompassed a diverse range of philosophies and perspectives. Accordingly, Zionists debated, and often disagreed, on numerous aspects, from the very nature of the movement to the timing, methods, and even the necessity of European Jews "returning" from their "exile" to the Land of Israel (Vital, 1980; Avineri, 1981).

Historians have closely traced the rich and pivotal Jewish intellectual discourse of pre-World War II Europe. However, their craft becomes more problematic and controversial when they shift their focus from the semi-theoretical political discussions in Europe to what "actually happened" in Palestine.

Pre-Zionism, the region was accompanied by an Arab population along with a long-settled yet small Jewish presence in the holy cities Jerusalem, Safed, Hebron, and Tiberias. Since the late nineteenth century, these Jewish-religious communities even began a process of expansion and modernization. Yet, the initial Zionist wave, spanning from 1882 to 1903 and known as the First Aliyah ("ascent"), consisted of approximately 25,000 people, symbolizing the start of a secular (and non-religious) Jewish presence in the "Holy Land." The Eastern European Jewish migrants in Ottoman Palestine were largely private farmers in agricultural colonies known as *Moshavot*, often eventually returned to Europe after enduring hunger and harsh living conditions in the Levant. Nonetheless, supported by the funds of the Rothschild family, they, among others, also established various settlements that ultimately grew into well-known major cities and towns in contemporary Israel.

The Second Aliyah (1904–14) was markedly more radical. Led by a small group of pioneers, constituting around 10 percent of the 35,000 Eastern European immigrants, who championed a revolutionary worldview, that, as noted by the astute historian of Zionism, Anita Shapira: "wanted a different Zionism, one that would be meaningful not only for the Jewish collective but also for the individual. It should embody a psychological revolution in the image of the Jew – a revolution of values, norms, and behavior" (Shapira, 2012: 43–4). Influenced by Romanticism and their Eastern European culture, the pioneers advocated for manual labor and the cultivation of the lands of *Eretz Yisrael* as the primary means of redeeming "the Jew from the malady of generations" and forming a "new" mental and physical fortitude (Shapira, 2012: 45). Although they only partially achieved their goals before 1914 and the outbreak of World War I, the pioneers succeeded in shaping the Zionist ethos, political leadership, and tensions that would influence Zionism (and the State of Israel) for decades – perhaps even until the present day.

Consequently, the Second Aliyah is widely regarded as the focal point of the Zionist Revolution and myth. We will revisit some of the historiographical interpretations of this pivotal and contentious period later on. However, the years following World War I were no less significant. In geopolitical terms, they were marked by the replacement of the four-hundred-year rule of the Ottoman Empire by the British Empire and the internationally governed Mandate system. With varying degrees of British support, Jewish society in Palestine, also known as the Yishuv (literally, "settlement") experienced extensive growth during the interwar years. The development received a significant boost after the rise of Nazism and the mass wave of hundreds of thousands of Jewish immigrants from Eastern and Central Europe, which almost doubled the Jewish population in Palestine.

By 1939, the Yishuv had already established much of the cultural and social infrastructure needed to govern a state. However, despite its many undeniable achievements, Jews in Palestine still constituted a minority in relation to both the overall local population and the worldwide Jewish population. In this context, Zionism remained far from its goals.

This status quo changed drastically after World War II, the Holocaust, and the end of the British Mandate (1920–48), when the newly established United Nations approved the partition of the land, effectively acknowledging the foundation of a Jewish state. Following this declaration and the departure of the British, the region quickly descended into chaos, leading to the 1948 War, the Nakba (the displacement of 700,000 Palestinians from their homes), and the declaration of the State of Israel. Historically, this Element seldom extends beyond the 1948 landmark. Therefore, this cliffhanger likely serves as a suitable point to conclude this short "chronological" survey.

However, historical narratives never unfold in isolation. As even my brief "neutral" historical background alludes, when shifting the historiographical focus from Europe to the Middle East, it becomes nearly impossible to overlook the presence of Indigenous Arab Palestinians. Even if we strive to concentrate primarily on the "Jewish side" of the puzzle, it is hard to deny that from the First Aliyah to the present, Jewish life in Palestine has been shaped by interactions with the diverse local population, gradually altering power dynamics and unintentionally turning the Jews from the oppressed to unwilling oppressors. Over the past thirty years, historians have extensively studied this consequence of Zionism. Nevertheless, the prism of our contemporary era also presents a less obvious and infrequently discussed historiographical challenge within the literature on Zionism: How can we, as historians working in the globally interconnected neoliberal second decade of the twenty-first century, write, imagine, and understand the people of the past?

Let me explain. Despite its numerous reservations about the Enlightenment and the *Haskalah*, at its core Zionism was fundamentally a modern movement that shifted the locus of power from God to man. This secular transition from a religious to a national and cultural community was entwined with another process: the creation of a "New Man," or, in the Zionist case, a "New Jew," often referred to as the "Hebrew." This aspiration, echoing to a certain extent the French and Soviet Revolutions, encompassed various subtleties, including messianic, gender, and social issues. Fundamentally, however, the Hebrew was a revolutionary attempt to break free from the perceived weaknesses, religiosity, illness, and passivity that supposedly characterized Jewish life in the "diaspora," replacing it with a robust, secular, healthy, and sovereign Jewish identity. Particularly since the Second Aliyah, the ethos of the Zionist "New Jew" emphasized a three-way intersection between language, body, and space as essential elements. The "New Jew," therefore, spoke a new language (modern Hebrew), inhabited a "new muscular" body, in a new space (the Land of Israel).

The impact of the "New Jew" on Zionism and modern Israel is nearly undeniable. In recent decades, however, cultural historians have tended to analyze it as a linguistic object, something that can be distilled to its core as a discursive web of representations and metaphors, and thus, ultimately dismissed as an excessive fraud, perhaps even a lie. Not entirely coincidentally, this methodological perspective became entangled in the historiography of Zionism with the post-Cold War globalized tendency to "deconstruct" old national narratives. Therefore, it is not utterly surprising that in the contemporary historiography of Zionism, the "New Jew" is currently understood as an elitist myth with only loose influence on daily life. Hence, like many other historical revolutionaries, the Jewish men and women who lived in Palestine are often portrayed either as morally inferior or, somewhat paradoxically, as a reflection of our own contemporary image.

This common liberal suspicion towards people whose ideologies, worldviews, and beliefs did not align with our current global-neoliberal focus on power, materialism, and well-being, is expanded upon in the next section. Yet, to a large extent, both the historiographical cynicism and nostalgia stem, in part, from what Eric Hobsbawm once described as "the snapping of the links between generations" (Hobsbawm, 1995: 15). It is within this current global-neoliberal gap between past and present that, in my view, the history of experience enters and reveals its full potential.

2 Experience: Emotions, Culture, and the History of Zionism

The problem of comprehending and writing about the foreignness of the past might have been overlooked by most historians of Zionism, yet it has received significant attention in the histories of emotions and the senses. While it would be fair to argue that, like global history, the emerging historiographical interest in emotions and senses reflects our current appreciation of the visceral as "authentic," the sub-field's basic presumption – that the meanings of love, pain, sound, change through time and place – also, often, leads to a fundamental objection to universalism.

Such concerns might be familiar to cultural historians who have been influenced by the scholarship of Michel Foucault and Jacques Derrida. Nonetheless, those mid twentieth century philosophers (and the numerous cultural historians who followed them), rarely wrote directly about emotions. That is not to say they ignored them, but rather, as a result of their comprehensive linguistic view, they perceived emotions as discursive-cultural side effects with inferior significance compared to issues of power, gender, and knowledge. Furthermore, In the aftermath of World War II, framing emotions as mere social constructs also alluded to the idea that vivid expressions of them were often considered brutish, uncivilized, and sometimes even fascistic (Rosenwein, 2002: 821–45).

Accordingly, a crucial departure in the history of emotions from cultural history is the presumption that emotions are not solely cultural constructions but are also derived from the body. This significant shift from the prism of cultural history, with its notion that "subjects are constituted discursively, and experience is a linguistic event," as famously argued by Joan Wallach Scott (Scott, 1991; 793), has recently been underscored by insights from neuroscience. By highlighting the interconnected nature of the sensory–emotional–cognitive process (Boddice & Smith, 2020), a determined group of historians has challenged the traditional Western Cartesian mind–body separation, redefining our understanding of the human experience. As Jan Plamper argued: "Experience is a central historical category waiting to be reclaimed for a holistic concept of social reality that overcomes false dichotomies of prediscursive versus discursive, unmediated versus mediated, embodied versus cultural, raw/visceral versus culturally/socially constructed, and ultimately nature versus culture" (Plamper, 2021: 141).

This is no light task. While the hundreds of milliseconds that separate sensation and perception may not seem significant to historians, according to cognitive scientists, it is a substantial amount of time for the body. Furthermore, although neuroscientists' empirical experiments are effective in measuring the senses, defining emotions remains elusive even in a laboratory setting. Thus, to the best of my knowledge, neuroscience offers limited insights into the changing historical meaning of concepts like love or smell. Last, but not least, even if neuroscience can prove the existence of the "prediscursive" and "unmediated," historians are still grappling with the enduring challenge of how to integrate it into their textual discipline. Despite all these challenges, however, the recognition that a portion of the human experience is embodied and visceral prevents us from fully reverting to the linguistic monopoly of cultural history. Therefore, above all, the history of experience encourages historians to reengage with their discipline and paradigms.

William Reddy's 2001 monograph, *The Navigation of Feeling: A Framework for the History of Emotions*, stands out as perhaps the most comprehensive attempt to establish a methodological foundation for the historical study of emotions (Reddy, 2001). In the more than two decades since its publication, the book has earned recognition as a pivotal work in the sub-field, and many of its new concepts, such as "emotives" and "emotional regimes," are frequently used and misused by fellow historians. Yet the book sub-title, concerning the *framework*, is often overlooked. Perhaps it is the current nature of historians to be more focused on the quickest path to the "production of historical knowledge" (whatever that may mean) and less on the mechanics of their craft. Yet, as Reddy himself recently observed, while doing so, they give up on the ambition "to go beyond the relativism common among cultural historians" and de facto treat emotions "as an aspect of cultural history" (Reddy, 2020: 168). This re-embrace of cultural history may be convenient and practical, yet it also *effectively shifts the sub-field from a methodology to a subject* without a clear definition or framework. The tendency to approach the history of emotions through the methodological assumptions of cultural history is frequently evident in the emerging studies on emotions in Zionism and Jewish history. Thus, it may be beneficial to briefly reemphasize Reddy's goal of transcending the limitations of cultural history and the methodological path it charts.

Published a day before the 9/11 terror attack – an event that, as Eelco Runia put it, "brought down the postmodern twin towers of language and meaning" (Runia, 2014: xiii) – *The Navigation of Feeling*'s point of departure is the author's desire to push forward beyond the relativism of cultural history. For that purpose, the first 140 pages of the book are dedicated to a theoretical discussion based on a survey of prevailing approaches to the study of emotions in the humanities and social sciences, as well as the limitations of the hegemonic paradigm of cultural history and poststructuralism.

Reddy is thus acutely aware that any exploration of emotions must grapple with the prevailing notions of the linguistic turn and the Saussurian concepts of signified and signifier. "The tendency in both structural linguistics and poststructuralism," he contends, "was to emphasize the limitations imposed by the structure of the system on what could be uttered or 'thought' by utilizing it. In the poststructuralist view, these limitations are so great as to rob utterances and texts of any independent significance whatsoever." This perspective, where "discourse determines everything that can be 'said' or 'written' within it," leads Reddy to believe "that the individual 'using' this structure to say something is robbed of all real choice, robbed of agency, reduced to epiphenomenal status" (Reddy, 2001: 87–8).

Against this weakness of poststructuralism, in which "there is nothing outside of discourse, language, or text," Reddy suggests the alternative approach of translation (Reddy, 2001: 93). "The concept of translation," he argues, "allows one to speak of the relation between language and the world in a way that is neither Cartesian nor poststructuralist. It allows one to say, meaningfully, that there are kinds of thought that lie 'outside' of language, yet are intimately involved in the formulation of utterances." "Emotions," he continues "are among the most important of such kinds of thought" (Reddy, 2001: 64). Hence, for Reddy, "the idea of extralinguistic, or nonverbal, thought material," is a crucial correction that allows "the possibility of human agency, of trial and error, as well as of a historical dynamic that has been sadly lacking in poststructuralist theory" (Reddy, 2001: 88).

Therefore, it is not coincidental that Reddy's test case for his framework is the French Revolution. Revisiting the "escalation" of the Revolution and the "Reign of Terror" in light of what he defines as the puzzling state of scholarship since the decline of social history and the rise of poststructuralist methods, the intricacies of Reddy's analysis, which include an examination of the evolving meaning of sentimentalism, are beyond the scope of this text. Yet, as *The Navigation of Feeling*'s final paragraph shows, Reddy's interest in the history of the French Revolution or the theory of emotions was always intertwined with an attempt to overcome the limitations of poststructuralism and cultural history.

Examining the political history of emotional regimes in France across the Revolutionary divide reveals that many French in the eighteenth century believed sentimentalism would guide them to a new and unprecedented kind of emotional liberty. This belief went to the scaffold with Robespierre, Couthon, and Saint-Just on 28 July 1794. The modern dualist conception of emotions, formulated in reaction against this stunning failure, lowered expectations, allowing greater flexibility, but at the cost of imposing a painful burden: a systematic, pessimistic underestimation of our capacity for self-determination. Poststructuralists revealed this pessimistic dualism to be a mere construct, but they threw out the baby with the bath water, selfhood along with subjectivity. The theory of emotives recovers for us a vast (if limited) sphere of endeavor, through which we may navigate with a full set of sails. (Reddy, 2001: 333)

As my brief analysis of *The Navigation of Feeling* has hopefully demonstrated, the book presents the history of emotions as a pioneering methodology throughout its entirety. A crucial yet often overlooked aspect of this analysis concerns Reddy's perspective on selfhood. By introducing the concept of a "disaggregated self," which moves away from Cartesian dualism to interpret "various codes or languages, both verbal and nonverbal," Reddy posits, in essence, that the self embodies a corporeal presence (Reddy, 2001: 95).

This is a drastic shift from the paradigm of cultural history, in which the body tends to be primarily seen as a mere image and byproduct of a discursive structure. As argued earlier, the acknowledgment of the existence of an embodied experience presents various questions for historians; yet, methodologically, it also pushes us away from engaging with historical selfhood and experience solely through the dominant method of deconstruction.

Often associated with its originator, Jacques Derrida, deconstruction holds a dominant position in the historian's toolkit. However, as Ethan Kleinberg recently claimed, "practically speaking, very few historians have attempted a serious engagement with Derrida or deconstruction for the practice of history" (Kleinberg, 2017: 1). Historians have instead widely employed deconstruction, a pivotal concept echoing the ideas of another prominent poststructuralist, Michel Foucault, aimed at "destabilization of authoritative pronouncements" (Kleinberg, 2017: 20). This gap between Derrida's concept and its popular use can be intuitively explained. While deconstruction is concerned with the unbridgeable gap between words (signifiers) and the things they refer to (signified), historians primarily see their discipline as arguing for "objective truth." Thus, if we endeavor to align more closely with the original concept of deconstruction, we, like Reddy, can highlight, for example, that the Cartesian dualism of mind and body is essentially a discourse with limited connection to "reality" (Reddy, 2001. 71). Others might even say that the current popular view of deconstruction is also very close to Hermeneutics of Suspicion and the writing of Nietzsche, Marx, and Freud (Ricoeur, 1970: 32–6). Yet, ultimately, the current amalgamation of the linguistic theories, poststructuralism, cultural history, and critical theory is frequently intertwined with an ethical/political quest to deconstruct notions of "power" (Doran, 2017). Thus, both the conservative and progressive advocates of this approach fundamentally assume that, like "truth" and "power," also "selfhood" and "experience" are something that needs to be decrypted by searching for clues and reading between the lines.

This tendency is notably evident in the contemporary cultural historiography dedicated to the modern Jewish life in early twentieth-century Palestine. Within the sub-field's internal terminology, the preference for cultural history over political and intellectual aspects is often associated with a wave of research that began in the nineties, labeled as the "Third Wave of Israeli Historiography" or the "Post-Post-Zionist Historiography" (Likhovsky, 2010; Kaplan, 2013). Advocating for the exploration of new and diverse historical voices, scholars adopting this paradigm often exhibit two interconnected thematic preferences: (1) an ostensibly "bottom-up" perspective that emphasizes individuals and groups, particularly in urban settings, and (2) the belief that Zionist ideology is not as pivotal to everyday experiences in both private and public spheres as previously assumed (Likhovsky, 2010: 9).

However, the embrace of cultural history in the 1990s also implies that "Post-Post-Zionist Historiography" did not solely arise from post-War social sensibilities but was aligned with the rise of Israeli individualism and the growing influence of right-wing populist political power. Consequently, "Post-Post-Zionist" scholars were less sensitive to theoretical concepts of poststructuralism or the distinctions between cultural and social history, while also embodying the impacts of rapid globalization (Appadurai, 1996). Thus, we can even argue that the predominant theme of their writing was the deconstruction of national ideology, under the assumption that "real history" would unveil a liberal selfhood committed to a familiar experience of materialism and well-being.

The worldview and hypothesis of the "Third Wave of Israeli Historiography" regarding selfhood and experience find notable representation in two scholarly works written in the early twenty-first century: Gur Alroey's *An Unpromising Land: Jewish Migration to Palestine in the Early Twentieth Century* and Anat Helman's *Young Tel Aviv: A Tale of Two Cities.* (Helman, 2010; Alroey, 2014). Both *An Unpromising Land*, which narrates the story of Jewish immigration to Palestine before World War I, and *Young Tel Aviv: A Tale of*, which delves into the city culture during the formative interwar years, received recognition within the sub-field (Alroey, 2004; Helman, 2007). Originally published in Hebrew, *An Unpromising Land* was lauded for "providing fresh insights into Zionist history and making it a must-read for anyone seeking to understand early Jewish immigration to Palestine," while *Young Tel Aviv* was hailed for being "the best among the rich array of new and exciting research on the history of Zionism" (Razi, 2011: 242; Wrobel, 2018: 324).

In light of this context, the endeavor to offer "fresh insights" and conduct "new and exciting research" was fundamentally an attempt to deconstruct Zionist ideology. In Alroey's *An Unpromising Land*, the stated objective is to reassess the myth of the Second Aliyah. Thus, instead of the "focal moment" of the Zionist Revolution, in which a small group shaped "the national ethos, the historiography, and the leadership" (Shapira, 2012: 33), the book portrays the 30,000 Jews that arrived in Palestine as participating in a modern, economically motivated migration period, that also brought millions to America

(Zahra, 2016). As Alroey himself puts it: "it was not Zionist ideology that drew these immigrants to Palestine but various prosaic motives, far less heroic than those described in Israeli historiography" (Alroey, 2014: 30).

Similarly, Helman's *Young Tel Aviv* aims to uncover the non-ideological everyday life in the first Hebrew city. Through a lively depiction of various aspects that encompassed the Jewish public sphere, such as events, leisure, consumerism, architecture, and hygiene, the book claims to provide a "reconstruction, description, and analysis of the origins of Tel Aviv's urban culture" (Helman, 2010: 4). Although Helman refrains from providing a clear definition of her use of the term "culture," the book's aim in adopting this "new" cultural focus is to go beyond society's "official formulations – those promoted by its leaders – and examine the incompatibility and even contradiction between what is said and what is done" (Helman, 2010: 7). For that purpose, Helman adopts a bottom-up approach that strives to separate the colorful and hedonistic "reality" of bourgeois daily life from the ideological and political portrait drawn by classical Zionist historiography. As one reviewer noted, the book "calls for a historical reevaluation of the Zionist project – an examination not of the socialist-utopian dream that was prophesied and desired but rather of the capitalist-bourgeois reality that actually developed" (Shoham, 2013: 432).

Thus, in many ways, this pair of books can be read as a series. In its first part, the poor immigrants arrive in Jaffa before World War I (Alroey), while in the second part (Helman), they find themselves in the comforts of the urban middle-class lifestyle of post-war Tel Aviv. Accordingly, in both studies, the "non-ideological" course of the historical experience is seen as stemming from a material logic that ultimately represents a teleology of well-being, where the rationale for all aspects of human activity and imagination is reduced to material aspiration and comfort. In *An Unpromising Land*, the downplaying of ideology as a key element in Jewish immigration to Palestine compels the author argue the Jewish immigration to Palestine was "generally the consequence of a difficult economic situation and a desire to improve one's standard of living" (Alroey, 2014: 103). On the other hand, *Young Tel Aviv* attempts to relegate ideology back to its "rightful elitist place," is based on a presumption that by doing so, the only possible outcome is a stereotypical, unchangeable, and familiar image of a hedonistic Western middle-class. As Helman notes, Hebrew entertainment and leisure culture "consisted largely of unsupervised imports of Western mass culture, with all its fads" (Helman, 2010: 157). However, is it sufficient to attribute the decision of Jews to relocate from Europe to an underdeveloped region in the Middle East solely to financial motives? If, indeed, public ideology and private selfhood are perceived as mutually exclusive, and the widespread Zionist desire to reshape the Jewish body, language, and space were merely a superficial influence on the "authentic" experience, how can we comprehend, for example, the Arab–Israeli conflict and the century-long history of Zionist violence, all purportedly in defense of their profound Jewish selfhood and experience?

In this regard, as the renowned philosopher Slavoj Žižek noted, "When some procedure is denounced as 'ideological par excellence,' one can be sure that its inversion is no less ideological" (Žižek, 1994: 4). Indeed, both books, published around twenty years after Francis Fukuyama famously declared the ideological victory of liberal democracy, serve as loyal representatives of the "end of history," signifying the ostensible divorce of ideology and experience (Fukuyama, 1992). Thus, the divisive modes of thinking about ideology and culture in Post-Post-Zionist Historiography hint at the formation of alternative overarching social structures that, in turn, serve as surrogates for the authors' ideology. Defining this new ideology is beyond the scope of this Element, yet I am reminded of a comment made by Eric Hobsbawm in 1995. While public institutions and collective behavior have yet to fully come to terms with the ascent of globalization, the old Marxist historian noted: "private human behavior has had less trouble in adjusting to the world of satellite television, email, holidays in the Seychelles, and trans-oceanic commuting" (Hobsbawm, 1995: 15).

In the face of this ideological standardization of imagination, the necessity of the inherited sensibilities of the history of experience becomes apparent. Let us take, for example, *An Unpromising Land*'s analysis of a 1914 letter sent by a potential Jewish immigrant, a druggist named Rabinowitz from the southern Russian city of Jekaterinoslav, to the Immigration Bureau (The Palestine Information Bureaus). The quoted part read as follows:

> Can a simple man known as a druggist open a pharmaceutical warehouse in Jaffa or in one of the cities of Judea and Gilgal? I am sick of my life in this land of new edicts, and with all my heart, being, and flesh I want to go to my ancestral land. But when such a thought occurs to me, a question immediately arises: What will you eat there, you and your household? After all, you aren't trained as a farmer, and commerce and manufacturing have not yet developed in Palestine. So what will you do there? I don't want to go hungry anymore, not even in our ancestral land (Alroey, 2014; 88–9).

In the source, Rabinowitz clearly states that he wishes to emigrate to his "ancestral land" with all of his "heart, being, and flesh." However, in *An Unpromising Land*, Alroey concludes that "if he [the druggist] was going to starve, it was better to do so in familiar surroundings than in a new country and in a strange society" (Alroey, 2014: 89). Such a reading is an interpretation imposed by the historian, as the question of "where to starve" is not explicitly or implicitly present in the source; on the contrary, the author expresses his explicit wish to emigrate to Palestine in order to live there, not to starve. Perhaps even more relevant to our discussion is Alroey's ignorance of the emotional and sensory elements of the text. Despite Rabinowitz's continuous use of bodily expressions to describe his emotional point of view, Alroey's analysis is centered only on the material, in which the body and the self are reduced to their physical needs – how not to starve. In a similar fashion, the expression "ancestral land" – "land of my/our fathers" in direct translation – is a fixed Jewish liturgical formula, symbolizing the traditional diasporic emotions of "longing for Zion." But where the Hebrew source simply reads "land" (*Erez*), Alroey translates it as "Palestine." Moreover, in the continuation of the source, which is not included in the book, Rabinowitz once again distinguishes life in the Land of Israel from "diaspora life" in Europe and the United States based on sensory-experiential connections when writing: "give us the ability to live there on its land and enjoy its sun" (Rabinowitz, 1914).

Another notable instance underscoring the pivotal yet often overlooked role of emotions and the senses is *An Unpromising Land*'s examination of Hebrew writer Chava Shapira's visit to Palestine. Originally published in 1911 as a series of articles in the Eastern European Jewish newspaper Hed Ha-Zman (The Echo of Time), Alroey highlights Shapira's reports as particularly "interesting because they describe the feelings of contemporaries and are not retrospective like later memoirs" (Alroey, 2014; 156). However, the glimpse into her impressions provided by Alroey is partial, concentrating solely on the ship's stop in the port of Alexandria before reaching Palestine. Consequently, *An Unpromising Land* focuses on the European surprise at the "shouts and noise" of a new world "where they were unfamiliar with his ways and customs," as noted by Shapira, as a sign of disappointment and a non-ideological perspective of the Jewish immigrants who arrived not in a utopia but in an underdeveloped land. Yet, while Shapira's description may carry a hint of condescension, it also reflects the joy of adventure, and it is Alroey who hints at the sensory significance of "the tumult, the shouts, and the pushing," indicative of "primitivism."

An even more striking example of the significance of emotions and the senses can be found in the parts of Shapira's reports that were excluded from *An Unpromising Land*, particularly in her depictions of Palestine. Already in her opening remarks, a few paragraphs before the description of Alexandria, she argues that a visit to Palestine is not for research or curiosity like a "regular trip," because "just the sound" of the name the Land of Israel "is enough to evoke special emotions (*Regashot*) within us as we approach that land we dreamed about since our childhood days when we began reading our sacred

books" (Em Kol Hai, 1911a). Similarly, after arriving in the port city of Haifa
and climbing Mount Carmel, she wrote:

> When you ascend this hill and gaze from a distance upon the entire city
> spreading before you, when you turn your eyes and see the Kishon River
> winding and meandering in the distance, and when you see the beautiful paths
> and streets, the olive trees and fig trees, planted on both sides, and the lovely
> flowers blooming among them – and above all this, the sky's azure, the bright
> eastern skies – then a feeling (*Regesh*) of pride sneaks into your heart, and you
> say, 'Indeed, our land is beautiful and magnificent!' (Em Kol Hai, 1911b)

In other words, Shapira's portrayal emphasizes the significance of being there.
She describes how, through the sensory experience of seeing the Land of Israel,
emotions are evoked. In the critical eyes of cultural history, this process will
likely be categorized and analyzed as hyperbole or manipulation. However,
Shapira continued this narrative when describing the Land of Israel in emotional
terms. "For the first time in my life," she wrote, "I felt (*hirgashti*) in
a completely Jewish atmosphere. The houses are Jewish houses on Jewish
land; the people, men and women, and the children, all of them are Jews,
Jews by spirit and soul. I felt this immediately as I stepped outside" (Em Kol
Hai, 1911b).

Certainly, one can argue that Shapira's printed reports are nothing more
than edited Zionist propaganda intended to mislead the reader, while others
might claim it is all just rhetoric, expressions, and metaphors, with little
historical value. Indeed, in some part, this is may be the case. However, the
main point is that Shapira, who never immigrated to Palestine before her death
in the Theresienstadt Ghetto in 1943, does not focus on culture or statehood in
her description of Jewish life in the Land of Israel; instead, she emphasizes the
senses and emotions. To put it simply, for Shapira, being in the Land of Israel
was an emotional experience. Similar "emotional prism" also appears in the
sources of *Young Tel Aviv*. Reading South African Zionist activist Marcia
Gitlin's 1933 impressions of the city, Helman is quick to highlight Gitlin's
initial disappointment with what she perceived as the city's "unattractive
exterior." However, by the end of her visit, as Helman pointed out, she
concluded: "Tel Aviv is not only alive but intensely alive." Thus, like
Shapira, also Gitlin, underscores the particular experience of the place. "It is
something that insinuates itself into one and gives one a sensation of complete
freedom. One is utterly at home" (Helman, 2010: 44). Gitlin's quote comes
after a long section in which Helman describes Tel Aviv's image as both
"lively" and ugly by Western standards. These clichés are still associated
with Tel Aviv today, as the city's unclean and noisy aspects are proudly

marketed in the slogan the "city that never stops." Yet, despite the welcome literary decision not to overly interpret the words of Gitlin and the many other protagonists of *Young Tel Aviv*, ultimately, the book's cultural perspective also reads those feelings as nothing more than a collection of images and representations. In this context, the book's methodology, which appears to align with what might be loosely termed Clifford Geertz's "thick description," primarily offers an overflow of anecdotes and trivial details while overlooking a crucial aspect: historical meaning.

Young Tel Aviv, for example, is full of the residents' complaints to the municipality about the noise of children playing in the streets, the constant car horns, and the sounds of radios blaring from open windows. Yet, as Helman repeatedly emphasizes, this urban experience was eventually embraced by the residents as their preferred way of life (Helman, 2010: 42). But why was that the case? Helman does not provide an answer to the question, thus neglecting the historical and emotional significance that Jews attach to the first Hebrew city, even when the sources suggest a more nuanced narrative. For instance, in the chapter on entertainment and leisure, Helman presents a domestic civil demand to the Hebrew municipality to extend the café's working hours. The letter from the café owner (omitted from the book's English version) once again emphasizes the connection between emotions and a Jewish space: "Here, in this city, the Jew feels himself free, always festive, and forgets his daily worries and misfortune" (Helman, 2007: 163). *Young Tel Aviv* briefly interprets the source as part of a domestic civil demand echoing "familiar" preoccupations of the petty bourgeoisie, disregarding the author's nuanced exploration of the literary nexus involving Jews, space, and freedom. Consequently, it overlooks the pervasive anti-Semitism, ingrained stigmatization of degeneration, and the profound sense of inherent otherness experienced by European Jews at that time. Therefore, *Young Tel Aviv* ignores that even a seemingly mundane act such as enjoying a cup of coffee as a self-assertive act in an autonomous Jewish public space might carry with it embodied and emotional meaning.

Thus, both books effectively captured the zeitgeist of their own time. *An Unpromising Land*, in particular, received praise for its originality, with one reviewer noting that it is "one of those rare, trailblazing studies that makes you wonder why no one ever thought to explore these matters before" (Shavit, 2004). To this day, their arguments enjoy widespread consensus and frequent citations in both Wikipedia and academic texts. However, in their analysis of "non-ideological" daily life, they both assumed that the sensory and emotional elements of the human experience are ahistoric concepts that do not change with time and place.

3 Hebrew Revival: Cultural History and the Experience of Language

Etymology is probably a good place to start a discussion on the historical Hebrew experience. The Hebrew word for experience, *havaya*, is a modern concept created by the influential Zionist philosopher A.D. Gordon in the early 1920s. First appearing in Gordon's pivotal book *Man and Nature (Ha-Adam ve'Hatavea)*, *Ḥavaya* is a portmanteau of *havaya* (being) and *ḥayyim* (life), which stands in juxtaposition with *hakara* (recognition or consciousness), a term with a strong association with culture in Gordon's thought.

For Gordon, *hakara* is external and restricting, while *havaya* arises from within, as an ontological moment in which "the world" is perceived by life itself. "This grasp of *havaya* is not a grasp of *hakara*," wrote Gordon:

> It is not the grasp (*hashaga*) of distinguishing what humans seeks to attain from within the boundless existence and concentrating it at one point, thereby making it clear and logical. Rather, it is a vital grasp, a grasp of expansion from what the human seeks to attain into the infinite, and therefore, it is not sensed (*morgeshet*) and not felt. Instead, it, through the concealed channels of *havaya*, maintains the absolute unity between what *ha-karah* centers at one point and the universal existence that extends infinitely. Through this, what is grasped by *hakara* is once again united with the infinite and lives in all that is infinite (Gordon, 2020: 162).

In short, *hakara* or culture is limiting and artificial, while *havaya* brings humans back to the boundless realm of "nature." In that perspective, Gordon's philosophy aligns well with the dominant ethos of the hegemonic Zionist pioneers of the Second Aliyah who advocated for the cultivation of the frontier lands of *Eretz Yisrael* as the chief element of the Hebrew experience. However, despite the inherent radical nature of the project, some parallels can be drawn between Gordon's *havaya* and the emotional descriptions of the Land of Israel by Gitlin and Shapira. In other words, as the contemporary historian Boaz Neumann argued, "Gordon granted Hebrew and Zionism the *havaya* of the Land of Israel" (Neumann, 2009: 230).

Thus, it is also not entirely surprising that, unlike other forgotten concepts invented by Gordon in *Man and Nature*, *havaya* is still a very common word in contemporary Hebrew. We will revisit its present uses in the epilogue when we attempt to see what has been preserved from Gordon's original meaning, yet, at this stage, it might be productive to emphasize that *havaya* is not directly equivalent to the English term "experience." First, unlike "experience," *havaya* carries an inherently positive connotation. As a linguistic editor recently informed a dear colleague of mine, the word pairing *havayat milhama* (war experience) is nonsensical in Hebrew. Second, just as German distinguishes, for instance, between *Erlebnis* and *Erfahrung* (which also exist in Yiddish and Russian), contemporary Hebrew also differentiates between *ḥavaya* and *nisayon* (the acquisition of personal or practical knowledge).

This kind of linguistic contextualization is a basic task for any historian attempting to bridge the past and the present. However, arguing that contemporary language can easily encapsulate Gordon's original meaning would be a slippery slope. We can note, for example, that *ḥavaya* overlaps, in many ways, with the contemporary Dutch historian Eelco Runia's definition of "presence," as "a moment of having a whisper of life breathed into what has become routine and clichéd – it is fully realizing things instead of just taking them for granted" (Runia, 2014: 53). We can also draw parallels between the Zionist Revolution's *ḥavaya* and Reddy's concept of "emotional regimes" – the normative order for emotions essential for any enduring political regime. Conversely, many Jews who arrived in Palestine seeking *ḥavaya* failed to fulfill their desire, experiencing what Reddy might term "emotional suffering" – a description of the mysterious act of translation that ended in failure, leading some to leave Palestine or even commit suicide (Reddy, 2001: 123). Thus, in alignment with Derek Penslar's recent exploration of love in early Zionism, we can ponder if, for some, it also manifested as unrequited love – the classic example of "emotional suffering" (Penslar, 2020; Reddy, 2001: 129).

But claiming that contemporary definitions allow us to fully comprehend the historical *ḥavaya* of being in the Land of Israel in the early twentieth century would be misleading. For Gordon, experience lies beyond culture and language. Thus, paradoxically, by attempting to describe something that transcends mere discourse, he effectively underscores the idea that words are not solely for straightforward communication but also play a vital role in shaping a holistic experience. Indeed, while Zionists still lived within Cartesian dualism, they often intuitively combined the body and the soul. For Zionists, the Hebrew revival (*Ha-Tehiya*) was intricately intertwined with the "revival" of the body and language. In this context, even the term "Hebrew" was frequently used as a comprehensive positive label for a new kind of Jewish existence, primarily in the Land of Israel. For instance, David Ben-Gurion, the future Prime Minister of Israel, wrote to his father:

> The Hebrew Renaissance, here it is! Hebrew signs on every store, Hebrew speech in the streets, stores, and restaurants, the buds of revival! No. Here you cannot doubt. You cannot disbelieve! [...] Here is a Hebrew boy riding with assurance on a galloping donkey, a Hebrew girl, eight years old, rides on a donkey loaded with freight – These are the visions of revival! (Harshav, 1993: 136)

Accordingly, Zionists persistently synthesized language, body, and space, asserting that the physical revitalization of the Jewish experience could only occur when Jews spoke Hebrew in the Land of Israel. For instance, Maccabi, the Zionist gymnastics club in Jerusalem, frequently translated textbooks and produced Hebrew dictionaries with the belief that mastering Hebrew was crucial for the "regeneration" of the body. Within this framework, they also consistently criticized accomplished Jewish-European athletes who did not speak the language (Idels, 2022).

Moreover, despite the contemporary confusion on the matter, the early twentieth-century Hebrew revival primarily involved transforming a written language into a daily life vernacular. For this reason, Zionists in Palestine criticized the old-European Ashkenazi dialect, the language of prayers, which was intertwined with Yiddish, the mother tongue of European Jews, and was full of "dipthongs like ay, oy, ey," which, for Zionists, symbolized Diaspora whining (oy vey, ay-ay-ay, oy-oy-oy). Instead, the range of Ashkenazi consonants dissolved in favor of vowels from the Sephardic (and ostensibly oriental) dialect, creating a minimal, direct, and straightforward language known as Israeli Hebrew. (Harshav, 1993: 165). The formation of Hebrew, therefore, had a clear sensory element, enabling people to hear it, see it, and, perhaps most importantly, express emotions in it. In simple terms, the Hebrew revival aimed to provide its new speakers with the ability to say: "I love you."

The difficulties of expressing "I love you" in Yiddish are the subject of several famous literary works in Yiddish. However, the Hebrew revival was also concurrently shaping a new modern Jewish experience (Peretz, 1888: 155). For many Jews, Hebrew was not just a set of fresh words, but served as their bridge to modernity and the wider world. Through the language, they engaged with fresh ideas and worldviews that were previously unknown to them, like, human rights, democracy, nature, and the names of animals and plants.

This transformation was not purely linguistic. When you give a red rose its name (*vered*) you also create a holistic connection between language, the flower's fragrance, and its symbolic context as "romantic" (Harshav, 1993: 92). As, Reddy observe, through the concept of "emotives," when we speak, we are not just describing but also doing things. Thus, for example, when we say, "I love you" or "I hate you," we are also producing feelings and emotions. In short, Hebrew not only provided the linguistic capacity to express "I love you" but also introduced new possibilities for feeling and experiencing it.

But this is also where things get a little bit trickier. Therefore, it may be beneficial to take a step back and briefly examine the Hebrew revival in a manner that allows us to recognize the significant role of the senses and emotions in this historical process.

Hebrew, as many contemporary critics and advocates of Zionism often mention, was never completely dormant before modernity. Nevertheless, it predominantly existed as a written language, rooted in the vocabulary found mostly in canonical texts. This collection of texts was to some extent familiar to Jewish individuals, who, unlike their non-Jewish counterparts, learned basic reading for liturgic purposes, with little regard to class or social status. Consequently, Hebrew primarily existed in a written form and as the recitation of oral traditions. Certainly, in rare cases, when two Jews lacked a common tongue, Hebrew might have been used as a spoken language. Nevertheless, such situations were not only infrequent but also severely limited in communication options when the vocabulary was steeped in religious contexts. I am reminded, for example, of a sketch of present-day comedian Elon Gold, which humorously illustrates that even after fifteen years of learning in an American Hebrew school, he could read the language but could barely speak a single sentence when he arrived in Israel (Gold, 2023). Hence, until the nineteenth century, when Jews spoke of *Mome loshn* (mother tongue), they were referring to Yiddish, Ladino, and various local languages and dialects. Conversely, Hebrew had no native speakers and was the mother tongue of no one.

Accordingly, no new oral sentences were created in Hebrew, the vocabulary was limited, and engaging in a conversation was nearly impossible, particularly on everyday topics like how to buy milk. As contemporary literary scholar Robert Alter noted, as even in its written form, as "a medium for representation of modern realities, whether social, historical, relational, or psychological," Hebrew was awkward and the artificial (Alter, 1988: 14). Simply put, the ability to articulate and convey the myriad ambiguities and complexities of the self and the human experience was practically non-existent.

Against this well-established and widely accepted historical background, the contested aspects of the "revival" narrative regard two main aspects: continuity vs. change, and the process's focal points and characters. The first aspect is the question of *whether modern Hebrew is a new language* or a continuation from biblical times. For the early twentieth-century Zionists, it was crucial to argue for the latter, as it was central to their revolutionary imagination to establish a connection between their existence and the ancient Jewish warriors who ostensibly lived and conquered the Land of Israel. This notion that Zionists speak a dialect of biblical Hebrew is deeply rooted in present-day Israeli culture. Thus, to this day, the secular public school system meticulously teaches how to read the Old Testament, and it is fairly common for novelists and journalists to claim that they write in the language of Joshua and the prophets. From a historical perspective, however, it is quite clear that modern Hebrew is a novel creation. As the prominent literary scholar Benjamin Harshav wrote,

Hebrew "was not an ancient language of a great ancient civilization, stagnant for hundreds of years (as Arabic or Indian cultures were), that is now gradually growing into the twentieth century; but rather a new language, recreated in the very heart of the transitions of modernity" (Harshav, 1993: 82).

And still, pointing out the novelty of the language or even, God forbid, suggesting any grammatical influence drawn from Yiddish, is still perceived by many Israelis as an invitation for provocation (Zuckermann, 2008). Thus, the idea that modern Hebrew is more a product of change rather than continuity is being criticized by both the conservatives (such as the Academy of the Hebrew Language), which sees themselves as the keepers of the torch of Hebrew, and Anti-Zionist leftists, who are glad to refute any ideological national myth. These vivid emotions and interests embodied in such discussions are an expression of the contemporary place of the language in the Israeli experience. But to understand the full influence of the innovation of Hebrew (as a creation of experience), we have to say a few words about the second, and surprisingly less contested, myth regarding the focal points and protagonists of the "revival."

The dominant narrative singles out Eliezer Ben-Yehuda (Perlman) as the main driving force behind the revival of the Hebrew language. Born in 1858 to a religious Yiddish-speaking family in Eastern Europe, Ben-Yehuda arrived in Ottoman Palestine in 1881. As one of the first immigrants of the First Aliyah (1882–1903), he settled in Jerusalem and dedicated his life meticulously to the revival of Hebrew. Up until his death in 1922, he established organizations and newspapers, wrote a historical dictionary of Hebrew (which he never finished), and coined various new words, many of which are still in current use. However, he is perhaps most known for his zealot nature and his militant decision to raise his son, Itamar Ben-Avi, solely in Hebrew, thus, making him the first Hebrew-speaking child but also condemning him to loneliness when forbidding him to play with other children who naturally spoke other languages.

Historians from both ends of the political spectrum resonate with this radical story. For conservatives, it fits the narrative of a self-made genius who led through action in the Land of Israel, while for liberals, it serves to generally downplay the ideological significance of the Second Aliyah (1904–14). However, it also has some flaws in its reasoning; to put it bluntly, learning languages just doesn't work like that. Even in our digital age of Duolingo, you can't revive, create, and certainly not learn a language in solitude. For such a "miracle," you need a mass of people who will immerse themselves in the language and all its aspects – reading, writing, speaking – a decisive volume that just wasn't available in Palestine or Europe during the First Aliyah. Even in 1914, the pharmacist Rabinowitz wrote in Hebrew that he wanted to learn to speak the language but wondered, "Who will I talk to?".

Indeed, Jewish schools in Palestine like the French *Alliance Israélite Universelle* and the German *Hilfsverein der deutschen Juden* taught Hebrew but only as a second or third language. Moreover, the teachers were not raised in Hebrew and often lacked the required expertise and knowledge for such a radical endeavor. Even Ben-Yehuda's Hebrew, as later critics tend to remind him, was artificial and limited, often forcing him to communicate with his wife using hand gestures, and more tragically, allowing his son to start speaking only at the age of four! (Harshav, 1993: 107).

This does not mean that Ben-Yehuda and the First Aliyah had no impact on the Hebrew revival. On the contrary, they made Hebrew an indisputable element of the Zionist cause, and proved that one can indeed speak the language. However, the key moment in the transformation of Hebrew into a living language occurred only at the start of the twentieth century, thanks to the Second Aliyah and, not less importantly, the renaissance of Hebrew literature that began in eastern Europe.

Beginning in the late nineteenth century, while Ben-Yehuda was already in Palestine, the Jewish renaissance was a modern, secular, and national endeavor that can be summarized as an attempt to write in Yiddish and Hebrew about all aspects of life and the world (Moss, 2009). Rooted in ideas that had originated decades earlier during the Haskalah, it reached its end after the establishment of communism and, eventually, the Holocaust. Yet, this remarkable cultural moment produced influential Hebrew writers and poets such as Mendele Mocher Sforim, Hayim Nachman Bialik, Shaul Tchernichovsky, Micha Josef Berdichevsky, and Yosef Haim Brenner.

Many of these canonical intellectuals eventually settled in Palestine, but already in Europe they had established Hebrew newspapers and wrote Hebrew fiction and non-fiction on diverse subjects. They translated Western classics into Hebrew, composed new original sentences in Hebrew, developed fresh syntax and grammar, and incorporated words and expressions from European languages (Harshav, 1993: 121). In short, when words were once lacking, substitutes could now be found or coined in Hebrew. As Harshav noted, thanks to the renaissance of Hebrew literature, "it became possible to write in Hebrew whatever could be expressed in European literatures" (Harshav, 1993: 123).

Nonetheless, the significant cultural undertaking of Hebrew revival was by no means complete. The transformation of Hebrew into a "living language" still required the intuitive usage of a native speaker who did not merely translate thoughts from another lexicon or rely solely on written sources. This transition, however, mainly took place in Palestine during the Second Aliyah and the British Mandate. Unlike the children of the First Aliyah, who learned their first Hebrew words in Palestine, the early twentieth-century "immigrants" were born into the Jewish renaissance and, thus, often read in Hebrew, covering religious, fictional, scientific, or philosophical topics. They also were more radical and ideological than the earlier settlers and less inclined toward integrating with the local Arab population. Instead, they aimed to establish "independent" Jewish spaces that symbolized their break from the Diaspora. In this spirit, alongside the pioneering colonies on the frontier, they founded Tel Aviv, the first Hebrew city. Two years later, in 1906, the first Hebrew school (Gymnasium) was established in the city. In 1913, during an event known as the "war of languages," it was decided that all Jewish schools in Palestine would teach all subjects (including math and science) exclusively in Hebrew. Such an "achievement" would have been impossible twenty years earlier.

However, this success does not imply the Jews exclusively spoke Hebrew. Even in 1916, demographer Roberto Bachi argued that Hebrew still wasn't the primary language for at least sixty percent of the Jewish population in Palestine. The gradual growth of Hebrew continued during the Mandate years, which, due to various waves of immigration, also saw linguistic diversity. In that respect, it is also important to emphasize that the prominence of Hebrew over Yiddish as *the* Jewish language largely occurred only after the Holocaust and the literal demise of the latter; but even in present-day Israel, various Eastern and Western languages are frequently spoken in both public and private spaces (Rojanski, 2020; Cohen and Levitan, 2023).

In short, while Hebrew was never the sole Jewish language, by the time of Bachi's survey, the revival had started to realize its aim of vitality. Consequently, even before World War I, Hebrew society and culture were emerging. Notably, in Tel Aviv, the colonies, and other "Jewish Spaces," children could be seen playing freely in Hebrew, perhaps for the first time in history. In 1912, Gordon wrote a letter to Hebrew writer Y. H. Brenner, describing this dramatic transformation:

> Today, it seems that there is no one with a rational mind who entertains doubts about the possibility of reviving our language in the land of Israel. We have become so accustomed to this vision of the Hebrew language, so accustomed to seeing its weaknesses and ridicule aspects within this vision, that we fail to realize that a great national creation is taking shape before our eyes and at our hands. But it's enough to go back just thirty years and look from there at the greatness of the living language in the land of Israel in order to be amazed by this grand spectacle. Hebrew schools in the full sense of the word, Hebrew gymnasium, that are not inferior in any way to any high school in the country … Many families speak Hebrew; it is spoken in the streets, in shops, and so on. Meeting, shouts, Hebrew visions, learning to speak Hebrew only from Hebrew, a nearly comprehensive understanding of the language. In short, a Jew who does not know any language aside from Hebrew, could almost effortlessly fulfill his linguistic needs in Hebrew.

Who would have believed it? Who would have dared to dream seriously about it thirty years ago! (Gordon, 1912)

The question of how something that not even a radical pioneer philosopher like Gordon would have "dared to dream seriously" about became a reality also leads us back to the emotional significance of the Hebrew language. Contemporary social and cultural history can provide us with some answers. However, even when they present all the "factual" dots, they are not always so easily connected, by stories of well-being or oppression. As Reddy claimed in his writing about cultural history and the Terror: "what it does not address is the question of how real people could have lived such an abstraction" (Reddy, 2001: 199). Against this "mystery" that transformed Hebrew into a living language, historical emotions and senses are essential. In other words, we need to consider Hebrew (or any other language) not merely as a tool for communication but as an integral part of a lived experience.

Such a prism, however, is unfortunately absent from recent cultural writings on the Hebrew revival in Palestine. As mentioned earlier, the issue I wish to highlight has a strict generational factor. Benjamin Harshav's *Language in Time of Revolution*, which, to a great extent, served as a basis for this section, might be also defined as cultural history. Yet, the narrative of the 1928-born Harshav does not attempt to deconstruct "authoritative knowledge," but to explain a vast historical event. Thus, Harshav, who was raised in Vilnius and experienced pre-Holocaust (Jewish) European culture, might not use the terminology of emotions and the senses, but he understands that the Hebrew revival was not just about vocabulary and syntax but a monumental event that drastically transformed the Jewish experience. "Hebrew was not simply a new language to supplant their first language while talking about customary matters." Harshav writes:

> Hebrew carried a whole new universe of discourse and a new semiotics, reflecting domains of life entirely new both to them and to the Hebrew language. The terms for nature and agriculture – the entire context of their existence – were unknown to them in any previous language; in those domains, Hebrew was their first language. Hence, the "conquest of the language" was intertwined with the "conquest of work," and with a new understanding of nature, love, the independence of women, armed self-defense, and a democratic or communist-democratic society. They learned all those new worlds of life along with the Hebrew words denoting them, which they uncovered or invented as they went along (Harshav, 1993: 150).

Nonetheless, the macro-historical perspective of Harshav's discussion also prevented him from presenting an abundance of micro "daily life" examples for the Hebrew revival. It is in this gap the scholars of "Post-Post-Zionist Historiography" aimed to make their contribution.

Let's take, for example, Arieh B. Saposnik's impressive 2008 book: *Becoming Hebrew: The Creation of a Jewish National Culture in Ottoman Palestine*. Attempting to step beyond the history of ideas and discourse, the book asks to "construct a bridge over the chasm separating vision, image, and discourse from praxis and concrete behaviors" (Saposnik, 2008: 5). Thus, unlike many of his colleagues, Saposnik does not wish to throw the "ideological myth" out of the window, but to "think about the implementation of those ideas and the ways in which imagination and discourse were translated (or transformed) into concrete institutions, customs, rituals, and the makings of an entirely unprecedented kind of Jewish life" (Saposnik, 2008: 6). As he writes in the introduction:

> It is no less important to recall that the people who compose those communities are not themselves metaphors at all and that they have very real lives in which the nation is encountered in concrete experiences. However complex, ambivalent, and disjunctive those experiences may be, it is through them that the nation has been able to play a defining role in the lives of those real people. The nation and the experience of it, in other words – however "imagined" and metaphorical they may be in many senses – are also rooted in observable cultural practices and in social processes that are very tangible and public and make up very concrete human lives (Saposnik, 2008: 5).

This is a promising start that the book largely fulfills. However, it also never defines what exactly constitutes an experience or "concrete human lives." Thus, ultimately, the book's cultural perspective is also limited to images, ideas, and the performance of national identity.

Following the premise that the Hebrew revival was a fundamental cultural undertaking of Zionism, *Becoming Hebrew* provides some fascinating and vital discussions on the Language Wars, early use of Hebrew in theaters and kindergarten, and, most importantly perhaps, the public debate regarding the first generation of Hebrew female speakers. Yet, despite acknowledging the temporal fragility of the historical moment, the cultural methodology, still, assumes that everything, including the body, is mediated through culture. Consequently, it overlooking the visceral and embodied elements through which language shapes the experience, and not less significantly, how the experience of talking, hearing, and reading Hebrew shaped the Jewish self. Thus, the book is less focused on exploring the experience of speaking a new language for the first time, and more on the various (and important) pubic discussions around this experience.

I am aware that it is much easier said than done, but without the emotional and sensory aspects of the Hebrew *ḥavaya*, the ability of *Becoming Hebrew* to describe the effect of the revival of language is limited to claims such as: [Hebrew] "was at once a representation and a vehicle for the creation of a 'Hebrew' national existence and for the emergence of a new generation of 'natives' whose language would be the basis for a sweeping transformation of Jewish existence," *or* that "so powerful a tool was the kindergarten in the eyes of its founders and advocates that it seemed to allow Hebrew's transformative power to penetrate beyond the public space of Jewish Palestine into the homes and family lives of its residents" (Saposnik, 2008: 84). In a similar descriptive style, Saposnik also turns to metaphors from the realm of astronomy:

> Zionism in Palestine was very much an attempt to reground language in mythological symbolic meanings and to re-create a Jewish cosmology that would have its feet set firmly on the concrete soil of Palestine and its head in a cosmos reenchanted to express the cosmic bond between the Hebrew language, the Hebrew land, and the new Hebrews themselves (Saposnik, 2008: 90).

All of those statements touch on the matter of things, but while the metaphor "cosmic bond" aptly reflects something that extends beyond our immediate understanding, it is ultimately, like "sweeping transformation," and "transformative power," figurative language that tells more than it shows. In light of this epistemological gap, much of the ontological dimensions related to the revival of Hebrew remain underexplored, and *Becoming Hebrew* can only capture a fragment of the profound and revolutionary experience of Hebrew life in early twentieth-century Palestine.

Such concerns are further accentuated in Yair Wallach's *A City in Fragments: Urban Text in Modern Jerusalem*. Published in 2020 and the recipient of the Association of Jewish Studies book award, *A City in Fragments* aligns with the objectives of "Post-Post-Zionist Historiography" by examining history through the lens of urban life and daily existence. It seemingly centers on urban texts, including "public notices, banknotes, street nameplates, visiting cards, commercial signage, government signs, and advertisements, which collectively made text an ever-present facet of the city" (Wallach, 2020: 20). Combining this "bottom-up" perspective with a multicultural narrative that encompasses the diverse experiences of the land's inhabitants, *A City in Fragments* attempts to offer a "creative and expansive history of the city, a fresh take on modern urban texts, and a new reading of the Israel/Palestine conflict through its material culture."

With this premise in mind, I looked forward to gaining insight into the Arab perspective on Jewish linguistic modernization from the book's chapter on Hebrew. Regrettably, to the best of my knowledge, the chapter contains only a solitary source representing an Arab viewpoint: the Lebanese intellectual Jurji Zaydan, who visited Palestine in 1914 and was notably surprised by the appearance of Hebrew texts on markets, shop signs, and hotel room numbers.

Even in this instance, however, the author ultimately assumes the role of spokesperson for Zaydan, suggesting that he "interpreted these signs as indications of an impending Jewish takeover of Palestine" (Wallach, 2020: 73).

Instead, the chapter titled "The Zionification of Hebrew" provides a political critique of using "god language" as a spoken tongue. The messianic aspects of Zionism and Hebrew have been extensively studied, as is evident, for example, in *Becoming Hebrew*. However, the book's attempt to draw an imaginary line between the secular revival of Hebrew in Europe and its Zionist contextualization ultimately misses the historical context. While it is true that many modern Jewish intellectuals did not take the daily use of Hebrew lightly, *A City in Fragments* displays a nostalgic longing for the days of the First Aliyah (a "Zionist concept" Wallach rarely employs). During this time, it argues, Hebrew was ostensibly both religious and modern, existing as part of a multilingual environment. Thus, overlooking that without the ideological revolutionary impetus of Zionism, primarily starting with the Second Aliyah, the radical endeavor of creating a new modern language might not have reached fruition (Wallach, 2020: 70).

The shortcomings of this cultural scholarly approach become especially apparent in the brief and singular paragraph where the book finally, and briefly, reveals to the reader that a significant aspect of the Hebrew revival was linked to its modern transformation into a vernacular:

> The Hebrew Revival's crowning accomplishment was the transformation of Hebrew into a spoken language. This enterprise, which took shape between 1903 and 1914, was led by educators in Jaffa, Jerusalem, and the Zionist colonies who taught children in kindergartens and schools, cultivating the first generation for whom Hebrew was a primary spoken tongue. The educators behind these initiatives were a mix of Palestine-born Jews and recent immigrants, Zionist colonists and urbanites, Ashkenazim and Sephardim. Hebrew as a spoken tongue bracketed out differences between these different elements and allowed them to think of their project as a national Jewish one. By the eve of the war there were several thousand Hebrew speakers in Palestine: children, teenagers, teachers, and committed enthusiasts. They constituted a small yet highly committed social base that would make possible the postwar Hebraization of Jewish communities in Palestine (Wallach, 2020: 73).

Thus, Wallach de facto acknowledges that the Hebrew revival was embraced by essentially all the secular Jewish sub-groups in Palestine. However, the linguistic project is still presented as a purely synthetic elitist undertaking, where people go to school to acquire a new language. The fact that just a few years prior it had a limited vocabulary, and no one, including the teachers, never spoke it, is therefore depicted as irrelevant. Moreover, the various human emotions and sensory elements that propelled the creation of a new mother tongue are reduced to condescending statements such as "allowed them to think of their project as a national Jewish one." In other words, the crucial ontological aspects of language, which apply to any language, are ignored. Hence, the Zionist's almost literal attempt to revive Hebrew in an intertwined desire to create a living language, a new Jewish self, and a novel living experience are left out of the story of the Zionification of Hebrew. Instead, they are replaced with a sterile view in which the physical existence of Hebrew is demoted to its most basic spatial presence as signs and billboards.

Much of these deconstructed historical experiences are drawn from the book's cultural methodology. After a long analysis of the theories of Derrida and Michel de Certeau, in the introduction, Wallach ultimately embraces the writings of German cultural critic Walter Benjamin, due to the "possibility of revolutionary awakening," in which "signboards and street names could be read against the grain; they could be used to write counter-hegemonic stories for the city and its people" (Wallach, 2020: 10–11). Given this narrow (yet hegemonic in the Humanities) critical view of text and history, it is less surprising that in the second half of the chapter, the author escapes from the loud and emotional streets into the comforts of literary analysis, theoretical discussion, and ana-chronistic sources (Wallach, 2020: 75–84).

Similar to *A City in Fragments*, Liora Halperin's acclaimed 2014 book, *Babel in Zion: Jews, Nationalism, and Language Diversity in Palestine*, also overlaps between cultural history and an un-mystified bottom-up approach. As Halperin writes in the introduction, the project "understands cultural history" as:

> incorporating a wide range of archival and published sources in order to capture the often nameless actors whose practices, decisions, and behav-iors, often on a local level, collectively constituted the linguistic land-scape and discourse of the Yishuv. The approach aims to reconstruct a cultural depth and complexity that is effaced by focusing on elites and emphasizing these elites' nationalist bona fides, and to reveal the lasting connections felt by Zionists, including supporters of Hebrew, to those languages and cultures that lay outside the communal boundaries of the Yishuv (Halperin, 2014: 19–20).

Building upon this perspective, Halperin aims to extend the narrative of Hebrew revival, which typically concludes around 1914, into the Mandate Period. Thus, *Babel in Zion* offers readers various and diverse anecdotes from daily life that unveil the multilingual reality in the thirty years leading up to the establishment of the State of Israel in 1948. Through acts of commerce, bureaucratic struggles, and visits to coffeehouses and cinemas, the book effectively demonstrates how Jews engaged with several languages in their homes, workplaces, and leisure activities. At the time it was a welcome and well-established addition to the scholarship, departing from the previous focus on "the study of the Yishuv as only the site of nationalist victory and pro-Hebrew cultural construction" in favor of "a society aware that it was negotiating language diversity and linguistic accommodation in more complex ways" (Halperin, 2014: 229). Indeed, as Harshav also briefly mentions, the prevailing scholarly assumption that Jews during the Mandate only spoke Hebrew was a misleading outcome of previous generations' ideological tendencies.

However, just like *A City in Fragments*, *Babel in Zion* approaches the history of Hebrew revival with an air of casualness. Despite being a nuanced writer who, at least on the surface, doesn't easily fall into the pitfall of assuming a "dichotomy between ideology and practice," but rather "seeks to understand the complexity of Zionist official discourse itself" (Halperin, 2014: 5), Halperin's introduction, gives only a quick, and abbreviated overview of the fundamental aspects the modernization of Hebrew. Briefly touching on notable figures like Ben-Yehuda and key events that unfolded before 1920, she argues that it was "a fairly typical late-nineteenth century linguistic nationalist movement" (Halperin, 2014: 6). While it is true that the Hebrew revival shares similarities with other nationalist movements, such a nonchalant treatment of the subject matter, where emotional statements toward Hebrew are dismissed as mere ideological rhetoric, ultimately creates a gap between history and historiography. Thus, devoid of sufficient context and an ear for the particularities, *Babel in Zion* often leaves the readers pondering whether Hebrew speakers came into existence through some kind of artificial laboratory creation or merely materialized out of thin air.

Paradoxically, this globalist worldview, in which languages do not have particular meanings, and thus, consequently, Hebrew is examined as just another "regular" language, also emphasizes the success of the revival's fundamental goal: to write and talk about everything in Hebrew. This normalization of Hebrew is evident, for instance, in the book's concluding remarks, where Halperin writes: "Languages in Palestine were tinged by economic as well as ideological pressures, personal as well as collective preferences. Languages could be symbols to be lauded, defended, or excoriated, but also tools for accomplishing real communication objectives" (Halperin, 2014: 229). She is undoubtedly correct; however, beyond the conventional academic juxtaposition of pressures and excoriation with "*real* communication object-ives," the absence of emotions in the survey also overlooks the possibility that the "real" meaning of Hebrew was not solely about exchanging words, but about creating a new self and living experience. Yes, Mandatory Palestine was a multilingual culture; however, does that directly imply there was a negotiation between languages? On the contrary, at least, from a purely globalized perspective, the diversity and popularity of other languages raise that question: how did young Hebrew ultimately prevail? Indeed, the rapid success of Hebrew was partially achieved by pressure from both the top and bottom. Yet, as Zohar Shavit noted, Jewish immigrants to Palestine were "required not only to adopt a language that had not yet achieved the capacity to answer all their needs but also to become active participants in its creation" (Shavit, 2017: 102). In short, Hebrew was more about choice than coercion. Thus, if one adopts a more existential and ontological perspective, in which languages are not merely a medium for communication, one can entertain the idea: the coexistence of multiple languages was not necessarily in opposition to the emotional and sensory significance of Hebrew in shaping and describing Jewish revolutionary selfhood and experience.

This prevailing tendency to overlook the connection between the Hebrew language and the Hebrew experience spans the entire political spectrum. In his 2000s essay "Towards a Hebrew Literature," published in the conservative Israeli journal *Azure*, renowned Israeli author Assaf Inbari strives to establish a framework for Hebrew writing. The essay stands out as a provocative and impressive piece of scholarship, urging Hebrew writers to return to the biblical writing style of "narrative prose," which Inbari considers the authentic form of Hebrew literature (Inbari, 2000: 100).

While the troubling political aspects related to crafting a narrative that comprehends time as "the flow of history, with humans as part of a nation, and reality as a series of actions rather than a constellation of objects in space" deserve exploration in another text, it is not surprising that, for Inbari, the point at which the "authentic form of Hebrew literature" was lost is the early twentieth-century "Jewish renaissance" (Inbari, 2000: 100). At this juncture, he argues, modern Hebrew-language literature shifted away from being historical, national, or active, now favoring individualism, descriptiveness, and being "immersed in the present" (Inbari, 2000: 127). In short, he concludes that Hebrew Literature was "abandoned in favor of language that represents the immediate experience of the present" (Inbari, 2000: 127).

Consequently, the essay's main villain is the most renowned and beloved author of the Second Aliyah – Yosef Haim Brenner. According to Inbari, Brenner's prose consists of "notebooks" from the immediate present, offering "static situations that contain almost no action but are rife with emotional agitation" (Inbari, 2000: 131). Without delving into the validity of the literary analysis, it is crucial, once again, to underscore that without Brenner and the Hebrew Revival, Hebrew – the language Inbari (and I) call a mother tongue – simply would not exist in its spoken or written form. Moreover, the modern language that Brenner and others created was always inseparable from the desire to forge a new Jewish selfhood. Therefore, the more "personal" writing style, which, as Inbari highlights, characterizes almost all Israeli writers, is not a coincidence or a wrong turn but a direct reflection of a group of people attempting to define and articulate the diverse and ambivalent feelings of their lived experience.

At this juncture, I believe my point is clear, and I may be becoming somewhat repetitive. However, when we shift from secondary literature to primary sources, we find that, much like Brenner's prose, speaking Hebrew was experienced as having a vital ontological *existence*. Let's return, for instance, to another part of Gordon's 1912 letter, in which he wrote to Brenner:

> Here lies a fundamental point, which is not given the proper attention. Here, creation unfolds, or revives, with the life force inherent in language. Many criticize the new linguistic creations in the Land of Israel without realizing that those who speak Hebrew in the Land of Israel, meaning those whose everyday language is Hebrew, are, in essence, in the same position – perhaps even more beautifully – as the writer who seeks to offer new ideas or feelings that have not yet found expression in words, and the language is not sufficient for them. Both the writer and the speaker do not seek to introduce a new word or pronunciation out of a desire to 'add to language'(*Lahaniach lashon*). It is the very force that compels the writer to create a new linguistic work that also breathes life into it, and it is that same force pushes the speaker to utter every word and breathe life into his creation. It is the force of life, the creative force within life (Gordon, 1912).

In order to embody this theoretical and somewhat abstract discussion, Gordon gives a simple example that retrieves Hebrew from the pages of the books to the most intimate and personal emotional experience between a mother and a child.

> If, some enthusiasts of a 'Hebrew language society' will renew a word like *oznei Haman* (hamentash, traditional Purim pastry) then the innovation would indeed be absurd and not beautiful. But imagine a woman standing in the kitchen, kneading and preparing a meal, while her beloved children, who know only Hebrew, stand around her and ask, 'Mom, what are you doing?' And if, out of affection, she decides to serve her beloved children, she answers them: You know, my children, today we are going to eat *oznei Haman*, then, the concept takes on an entirely different essence – a vitality of life. It doesn't matter that the word is neither beautiful nor accurate – perhaps over time, a more beautiful and accurate word will be found . . . and even if it isn't found, it's not so terrible: in the linguistic realm exist words that are neither beautiful nor accurate. The main thing is that the living concept will find a living expression (Gordon, 1912).

Some might argue that due to Gordon's association with the pioneers of the Second Aliyah, we should treat his statements with caution, as they may be perceived as ideological. Perhaps. However, Hebrew writer Micha Josef Berdichevsky, who never lived in Palestine, wrote around the same time: "What makes a tongue special is not simply its expressions and sounds, or indeed its euphemisms and content, but its quality, or more precisely, the character of those speaking said tongue, those born into it, who began seeing the world, thinking and feeling, but also fighting and socializing through it." (Berdichevsky, n.d.). Another influential *Ha-Tehiya* writer, Hayim Nachman Bialik, made a similar statement when arguing, "want everyone to do everything in Hebrew ... shit in Hebrew, shout, steal, commit adultery in Hebrew" (Shavit, 2017: 133).

The perception of language as a living experience also appears in Bialik's famous 1915 essay, *Revealment and Concealment in Language* (*Gilui vekisui balashon*). While discussing the meaning of words and language, the Zionist national bard does not explicitly mention the Hebrew Revival. However, akin to Gordon, he advocates for a rejection of a mere linguistic understanding of the human experience. "It is clear that language in all its forms does not admit us to the essence of things," wrote Bialik, "On the contrary, it serves as a barrier against this essence." In short, Bialik does not take it upon himself to articulate a *ḥavaya* that will bridge between culture and nature but acknowledges that "on the other side of the barrier of language, behind its curtain, stripped of its husk of speech, the spirit [*ruach*, also soul] of man wanders ceaselessly" (Bialik, 1950).

Against this tragic verdict, in which humans' ability to express and understand their experience has been thwarted by language and culture, Bialik chooses to end the essay by providing a glimpse of hope:

> So much for the language of words. But, in addition, "there are yet to the Lord" languages without words: song, tears, and laughter. And the speaking creature has been found worthy of them all. These languages begin where words leave off, and their purpose is not to close but to open. They rise up from the void. They *are* the rising up of the void. Therefore, at times they overflow and sweep us off in the irresistible multitude of their waves; therefore, at times they cost a man his wits, or even his life. Every creation of the spirit which lacks an echo of one of these three languages is not really alive, and it were best that it had never come into the world (Bialik, 1950).

Bialik's concluding remarks bring us back to the realm of emotions and the senses, invoking feelings of song, tears, and laughter. He transports us to a place where language and humanity are not isolated in a cultural vacuum but rather open, engulfing us in the irresistible multitude of their waves, like a parent offering a sweet treat to a joyfully playing child. They return us to the realm of lived experiences, where language and humans are "really alive."

These deep philosophical discussions have also influenced and reflected public and personal aspects of the Hebrew revival and experience in Palestine. In my work on the rise of "Jewish sports" in interwar Palestine, for instance, I pointed out the link between the ambivalent Zionist reading of the sporting experience and its particular linguistic description in the Hebrew press (Idels, 2022). However, other examples abound and go beyond the limited scope of this Element. Therefore, it would be perhaps fitting to conclude this section with another excerpt from Chava Shapira's 1911 visit to Palestine, in which she describes the emotional bond between the Hebrew revival and the Hebrew experience:

> Many were the impressions I received in the Land of Israel, but the strongest and most joyful was when I stood amidst the semicircle of singing girls. These healthy Hebrew children, all filled with the same Hebrew soul, free from any external or internal burden, reciting verses of about their land and soil – is there more heartwarming sight [. . .] The Land, the azure sky, and the delightful nature, I felt them here more deeply, standing beneath the heavens, with the refreshing and melodic voices resounding and rising. To be a free people in our land, and from afar, the voices of other children joined them, drawing near [. . .] The children play in Hebrew – and the conversation is so natural, *so alive!* Come now – I thought – all those who claim that the Hebrew language is dying and has no future, come and listen to the joyful chatter of these little boys and girls playing here, and deny the possibility of the revival of Hebrew speech! (Em Kol Hai, 1911b).

4 Eating the Grain: Reading Sources, Ethics, and Receptiveness

Shapira's text is rich with descriptions of senses and emotions. As I have endeavored to demonstrate in the preceding section, the recent disregard of cultural historians for the emotions and senses intertwined with the Hebrew revival often results in missing significance historical context and meaning. Shapira's text, however, serves as a historical source. Therefore, when it becomes part of a historiographical narrative, it inevitably undergoes a process of interpretation. One popular approach is to read the text against the grain, often arguing that it is nothing more than a collection of metaphors and images, offering little evidence for understanding "what actually happened." In this nominalist view, language is considered a barrier to the historian's quest for "truth." The essence of this "truth" may vary, depending on the narrative ethical and political perspective, regarding Zionism, the region, and history. In the case of *Unpromised Land*, economic considerations take precedence, while for *A City in Fragments*, it is about power, and for *Young Tel Aviv* and *Babel in Zion*, the focus is on well-being.

However, despite this array of opinions and interpretations, by refusing to engage with the text, they inadvertently impose a contemporary "rational" perspective on the past. That is, they assume that text like Shapira's descriptions of the profound feelings she experienced while "standing beneath the heavens, with the refreshing and melodic voices resounding and rising" are mere rhetoric or empty language, devoid of "real" historical meaning. As anthropologist Paul Connerton outlined in his 1989 classic *How Societies Remember*, "Historians investigate evidence much as lawyers cross-question witnesses in a court of law, extracting from that evidence information which it does not explicitly contain or even which was contrary to the overt assertions contained in it." "Historians," the British anthropologist continued "are able to reject something explicitly told them in their evidence and to substitute their own interpretation of events in its place. And even if they do accept what a previous statement tells them, they do this not because that statement exists and is taken as authoritative but because it is judged to satisfy the historian's criteria of historical truth." "Far from relying on authorities other than themselves," Connerton concludes, "to whose statements their thought must conform, historians are their own authority; their thought is autonomous vis-à-vis their evidence, in the sense that they possess criteria by reference to which that evidence is criticized" (Connerton, 2009: 13).

While many historians may disagree with this statement, for Connerton it is a necessary step in understanding memory and recollected knowledge of the past that is conveyed and sustained within the body. Thus, while *How Societies Remember*, with its emphasis on performance and ritual, may differ from the current writings of historians of emotions, such as Reddy; it, nonetheless, acknowledges the importance of the non-textual aspects of history, which are intertwined with the limitations of the historian's "scientific practice." "Historians continue to question the statements of their informants," he wrote, "because if they were to accept them at face value that would amount to abandoning their autonomy as practising historians" (Connerton, 2009: 14).

But is it truly the case that historians must always read against the grain? Or is it possible for them to accept their sources at face value without "abandoning their autonomy as practicing historians"? Indeed, as Paul Connerton pointed out, even the fundamental processes of gathering and selecting evidence involve a degree of interpretation. This interpretation extends to the selection of subjects and timeframes, and, as Hayden White argued, even to the inherent act of narrativization that is at the core of a historian's "scientific practice." In short, the writing of history fundamentally involves interpretation and contextualization. Paradoxically, however, it is precisely within this inescapable literary act that, in my belief, the enigma of the historical experience should be engaged. As Hayden White once wrote, "The best counter to a narrative that is supposed to have misused historical memory is a better narrative." By this, he meant a narrative not filled with more historical facts but one that possesses "greater artistic integrity and poetic force of meaning" (White, 2005: 336).

Thus, interpreting Shapira's texts not as exaggerated or false but as testaments to an experience that we, the people of the present, cannot fully grasp, is not a methodological dead-end, but an acknowledgment of the inherent difference of the past. For me, this abstract and ambivalent literary space, where past and present collide but never fully coalesce, is where the history of experience truly shines. As Thomas Dixon writes:

> The history of emotions has the remarkable ability to allow us not only to see but also to feel both sameness and difference, connection and distance in relation to our fellow humans. An inconceivable variety of sentiments and affections have stirred human bodies and minds in the past [. . .] Nevertheless, historians of emotions and their subjects remain beings of the same species, possessing similar powers of the mind (Dixon, 2023: 19).

One might argue that the sub-field's essential goal to enable us to see and feel both sameness and difference is ultimately restricted by the constraints of scientific writing. However, the crucial word here is "difference," which can also be described as diversity. Or, as cultural historians once argued, "other people are other" (Darnton, 2009: 4).

Characters, as post-critique scholars have recently noted, are a key element in fostering the reader's attachment to literature (Anderson, Felski & Moi, 2019). "These figures," writes Rita Felski, "are not merely bundles of signifiers; they are worldly actors haloed with affective and existential force" (Felski, 2020: 89). This is particularly true in the case of historiographical portrayals, especially since, as Felski emphasizes, identification and attachment do not equate to sameness. "Characters," she contends, "are fascinating not just as prototypes or models for real-world interaction but because of their difference – their aesthetic difference" (Felski, 2020: 86). Conversely, historians tend to frame their subjects within a theoretical or conceptual framework, which may portray their historical protagonists as "rational" or "logical" to the reader. This prism can be explicit or implicit, conscious or unconscious; it can view and judge the people of the past as both good and evil. However, it is rarely assumed that we can't understand and interpret them.

However we can't fully fathom what Shapira felt that day amidst the semicircle of singing girls. Perhaps her allusion to joy (*Oneg*) hints at a path to historical contextualization. Yet, this significant endeavor also remains confined, as even in her detailed description explicitly linking her experience to being "free people in our land," the mystery of the past endures. The "melodic voices," once resounding and rising, have long faded away, and the meanings of the fleeting feelings of "the Land, the azure sky, and the delightful nature" elude our grasp. And still, such an emotional statement does not lead historians to an impasse but extends an open invitation to listen and immerse ourselves in the diverse and abundant experiences of the past.

Boaz Neumann's *Land and Desire in Early Zionism* stands as the most significant, and perhaps the only, scholarly endeavor to embrace such a perspective in the historiography of Zionism (Neumann, 2011). Initially published in Hebrew in 2009, the portrayal of the Zionist pioneers (*halutzim*) "daily life" was considered an integral part of the emerging "Third Wave of Israeli Historiography" – a term Neumann himself even coined (Likhovski, 2010: 2). Nevertheless, the book's description of the pioneers' relationships with the land, body, and language sets it apart from the rest of the "Post-Post-Zionist Historiography." Not only does Neumann's focus on the men and women of the Second Aliyah distinctly differ from the generally urban settings of Post-Post-Zionist literature, but it also boldly centers the narrative around the pioneers' "ideology." In contrast to almost all Zionist historiography, Neumann's introduction states, "[the book] presents the pioneers' most central experience – the existential reality of being in the Land of Israel and their basic desire for the Land – without reducing this desire, as most historians do, to a political, economic, romantic, or psychological phenomenon" (Neumann, 2011: 13). In short, Neumann deliberately chooses not to deconstruct.

The book's central theme is desire. Neumann's offers the reader a comprehensive theoretical definition of it, but he also acknowledges its elusiveness, stating, "I do not intend to explain the pioneer desire for the Land of Israel. Attempts to explain the causes and sources of this phenomenon, as well as its purpose, miss the mark. Instead of explaining, I seek to describe" (Neumann, 2011: 14) In line with this approach, the book is replete with descriptions of the pioneers' experiences, many of which may seem peculiar and foreign to the contemporary liberal mindset, much like Shapira's text. For instance, concerning the Hebrew revival, Neumann cites a pioneer who mentions the Hebrew expression "a breeze that restores the soul" (*Ruach Mesheevah Nefesh*): "used to be strange to me, but when I was 'soulless' and the breeze came and returned it to me, I said: I want the breeze to return again and again and 'restore my soul'" (Neumann, 2011: 234). Similarly, he quotes pioneers who felt that while working the land, God spoke to them: "Here they walk in the furrow, and He [God] speaks to them from the furrow, from the sprouting, burgeoning field, from the gold of the grain field as evening falls" (Neumann, 2011: 239). This emotional experience is further elaborated in another quote: "When the divine presence (*shekhina*) permeates you, you are focused within yourself, and all the clamor around you that reaches your ears is but a distant echo, like the song of the birds in the forest or the croaking of the frogs in the marsh. Sounds indeed strike the eardrum, but one simply senses the harmony that makes them part of the song of the entire universe – the song that awakens and lifts the soul higher and higher, taking pleasure and dissolving in longing and in pleasure" (Neumann, 2011: 239).

These are indeed powerful texts, but it is still Neumann's decision to read them not merely as sublimations or metaphors for other feelings or needs but as evidence of a historical experience. This literary choice is also, and perhaps inevitably, intertwined with an understanding of language itself as an embodiment and visceral medium. Thus, in response to the common scholarly claim that the pioneers' rhetorical excess, both in terms of quantity and quality, created a distorted view of historical reality, Neumann argues that there is no need to prune and purge the language to reach "historical truth." Instead, he suggests that we should not differentiate between the concrete practices of the pioneers, such as physical labor, road construction, and settlement building, and their use of language. Rather than regarding speaking and writing as practices with different epistemological and ontological statuses – namely, as false or at least manipulative – he recommends placing them at the center of the history in which they unfolded. "These works of literature are an integral part of the pioneer desire for the Land of Israel, necessary components of pioneer praxis," he concluded, "Plowing the earth is no more or less important, 'true,' or concrete than a poem about the soil" (Neumann, 2011: 250).

Accordingly, it is also Neumann's decision to accept language at face value that grants the sources an historical and historiographical significance. By reading the pioneers' texts as evidence of existential experience, *Land and Desire* complements, for example, *Becoming Hebrew*'s use of figurative language, such as "cosmic bond" and "transformative power," while also effectively fills the void left by Harshav's top-down approach by showing the pioneers' unwavering commitment to the Hebrew revival.

Moreover, such a reading enables a particular ethical reflection on the past and present. Writing after the escalation of the Arab–Israeli conflict during the early twenty-first century (the Second Intifada), Neumann's ambition for his journey into the historical pioneer desire is the feeling that the common liberal "rational" prisms do not provide a sufficient explanation for the bloody chaos of his time. "The genesis of this book," he writes in the preface, "lies in an intuition that, in order to explain aerial bombing missions and exploding buses, we must look beyond politics, economics, ideology, history, and religion" (Neumann, 2011: ix). In that respect, Neumann not only clearly acknowledges the troubling and dreadful consequences of the pioneers' existential act but also grants the text an ethical perspective that transcends most of the academic discourse.

Thus, despite the Arab population being mostly absent from the narrative, *Land and Desire* succeeds where other "normative" and ready-made theories fail. Where historians tend to reflect on the violence as a teleological outcome of nationalism or colonial power, Neumann poses the most basic and human question: why do Jews and Arabs exhibit willingness to commit acts of ferocity and sacrifice? "I call that something desire," he answers, "by this I mean the desire of each party to the conflict for this land, a desire that, in clashing, leads both parties to disaster" (Neumann, 2011: ix). Also, for the second half of the equation, where reciprocal history ostensible shines as the only option, "a description of Palestinian desire for this land," Neumann concludes at the end of the preface, "can be produced only by a Palestinian" (Neumann, 2011: 11).

Such an ethical reading may be foreign to the current academic fashions, yet it unveils a tragic and intricate narrative that defies simplistic notions of right and wrong. Instead, it weaves a nuanced – and human – historical account of the pivotal moment when the Hebrew experience was born, and the very essence of Zionism became inseparable from the physical presence in the Land of Israel. *Land and Desire* closes with a historical pioneer illustration, envisioning a century later when a teacher would guide pupils to the region of Zionist settlements, using a "magic lantern" to depict scenes from the lives of their ancestors:

> After lunch. The day blazes like a furnace, a man covered in sweat and dust sits on a machine and plows. Suddenly Arabs appear on all sides, armed, large and small, with clubs, stones, knives, and pitchforks, acting as if they want to attack the plowing man ... The camp of the attackers approaches him and it looks as if they will soon tear him to shreds, but suddenly they all turn around and retreat in their tracks
>
> "What is this?" the children ask excitedly. "Those are the Arabs who wanted to frighten our forefathers from settling in this place, but they failed" (Neumann, 2011: 252).

This text was written in October 1924. Ninety-nine years later, in October 1923, the Zionist and Palestinian desires appear stronger and more ferocious than ever.

Regrettably, *Land and Desire*'s contributions have been largely overlooked. Despite being translated into English and receiving relatively broad exposure, the book was mostly ignored or criticized for its emphasis on the Second Aliyah pioneers as the pivotal moment in Zionism (Alroey, 2010). Consequently, historians have deliberately disregarded many of *Land and Desire*'s methodological perspective it offers on history and language over the decade since its publication, favoring materialistic and somewhat cynical approaches that predominantly consider power and well-being as the primary "empirical" and "analytical" evidence of historical experience.

Accordingly, the scholarly possibility of approaching historical sources with a receptive ear has been largely overlooked by scholars of Zionism in recent years. However, the current emergence of the history of emotions in the sub-field rightfully recognizes *Land and Desire* as one of the founding works in this area (Penslar, 2023: 259). Thus, we can hope that the growing interest will also consider some of the suggestions made in the book regarding language and experience. Yet, considering that the majority of the initial work on Zionism and emotions is being conducted by cultural historians who view their role as deconstructing myths and challenging authoritative power, I have my doubts, but only time will tell.

In that regard, it is essential to emphasize that the reading of the history of experience is not primarily based on empathy. On the contrary, the history of emotions tells us that empathy itself is historical (Barclay, 2022). Therefore, arguing that we can empathize with the people of the past constitutes a form of liberal condescension. Rather, comprehending and sharing the feelings, thoughts, and emotions of people from the past is practically impossible, and while some essential linguistic contextualization can be achieved, the visceral essence of the experience is often lost in the sands of time. However, whereas attempts to achieve imaginary empathy are doomed to fail, *receptiveness* allows historians to embrace the diversity of the past.

Listening does not equate to identification or acceptance. The other can embody both goodness and evil. Receptiveness is about being open to the emotions, beauty, and pain of the ever-changeable human experience. It is an acknowledgment of the fragility of our own era, that possesses "zero nostalgia for the past but hopes for a less cynical and disenchanted future" (Felski, 2020: viii).

This kind of reading and writing recognizes that historical narrative is never entirely separate from questions of ethics in historiography. The ethical implications of writing history always depend on how information is contextualized through its organization, even when dealing with morally self-evident issues. As Hayden White notes, "[o]ur knowledge of the Holocaust could hardly be more complete or more compelling in regard to its 'facticity'; what we need are imagination and poetic insight to help us divine its meaning" (White, 2005: 338). In short, White tells us history writing is more about meaning than mere knowledge.

Thus, it is not coincidental that White doesn't advocate for understanding meaning but rather for divining it. He suggests an openness to the past "quite different from morality that, on the basis of some dogmatism, insists on telling us what *we must and must not do* in a given situation of choice" (White, 2005: 338). This departure from pseudo-scientific attempts to uncover "what happened" is, as

White explains, "ethical in that its subject-matter (violence, loss, absence, the event, death) arouses in us the kinds of ambivalent feelings, about ourselves as well as about the 'other,' that appear in situations requiring choice and engagement in existentially determining ways" (White, 2005: 338). The intersection of experience and White's "postmodernist scholarship" might seem paradoxical to many historians of emotions. Yet, for me, in this ambivalent nexus where literature, history, and ethics converge into narrative, the histories of emotions, senses, and experience can transcend cultural boundaries. This is the place where the history of Zionism can be illuminated, and Israelis can once again ask questions about their ancestors and themselves, not through the lens of nostalgia or cynical hatred but with postcritical faith filled with love and fear.

5 A Brief Epilogue on the Emotions of Past and Present

The questions of how and why to engage in the writing of history are never self-evident. This Element, therefore, does not advocate for a new theoretical dogma to be automatically adopted; rather, it invites a reflective inquiry into historiographical trends often considered absolute and definitive, with the hope that historians will continuously contemplate and reassess the essence of their peculiar profession. In particular, it focuses on the assumptions and questions that the histories of emotions, senses, and experience can offer. The current popularity of these fields is unsurprising in our time, where, as Hans Ulrich Gumbrecht has noted, there is a "renewed concern with the physical aspects of human existence" (Gumbrecht, 2014: 21). Indeed, the writing of the history of emotions may be akin to contemporary obsessions with food and jogging, yet, this statement should not necessarily be viewed as criticism but as a reflection that history is always written from and for the present.

Yet, the methodological issue of how to write the history of something as abstract yet tangible as emotions and the senses remains unclear. One potential approach is the expansion of the realm of creation. Few, I believe, would disagree that a historian's product can encompass more than the occasional black-and-white photo or the synthetic sound of a PowerPoint presentation. Especially now, in the emerging age of A.I., the possibilities for creation are greater and richer than ever before. However, technology does not address the pivotal questions of how and why we tell the narratives we call "history." Christopher Nolan's 2020 blockbuster film, *Tenet*, for instance, was a perplexing sci-fi exploration of the experience of time. Despite being perhaps the most analytical of all mainstream directors working today, Nolan advises his protagonist and the audience at the start of the movie, "Don't try to understand it, feel it." The film's fans, however, didn't always heed this advice, and the web was filled with diagrams and videos attempting to decipher the film's many intersecting timelines and alleviate their confusion. Similarly, professional historians tend to advocate for understanding the past. Shielded by the sterile and clean textual dimensions of their craft, they eagerly protect their "scientific" monopoly to decide "what really happened."

However, could historians also benefit from embracing the unknown? I once met a curator working on a historical exhibition about the senses. When I asked if they had ever attempted to recreate the smells of different historical periods, he replied, "Yes, we did, but the audience couldn't tolerate it, so we had to stop." It remains uncertain whether the scents produced in the museum accurately represented, for instance, the historical odors of the eleventh and twelfth centuries. Yet it suggests that some things should remain a mystery. Historians usually don't like unsolved questions much. Particularly in today's context of deconstruction and the hermeneutics of suspicion, academic historical writing often revolves around uncovering the past and distinguishing it from ostensible myth. Even the current trend in the history of emotions and the senses focuses on forming a new "analytic" and "scientific" terminology by "systematically" and "critically" engaging with the past through new conceptualizations. Yet, no concept or framework can overcome the fact that if we assume that the human experience is not merely linguistic, something has been irrevocably lost to the passage of time in its transition to text. Thus, the predominant question is what to do with the text itself: rationalize it, deconstruct it, explain it? Or perhaps, we can also read it not as a cryptic puzzle demanding analytic decryption but as a voice from the past that we can listen to carefully but never fully understand.

Such a reading should never be made in an anachronistic vacuum. Yes, context is important, and some historians do know a lot about the social and cultural reality of various times and spaces. But we should also not fear, and might even cherish, moments of cognitive impasse, in which simple answers cannot be given, and the reader is inclined to think about himself and the other.

In literary terms, such a perspective might suggest moving away from jargonistic discourse that aims to simplify, organize, and comprehend, opting instead for a direct language that endeavors to describe the ineffable. Critics might contend that this "artistic" return to the humanities risks pushing the boundaries of the discipline, potentially shifting its focus from "objective" argumentation to conjecture. However, other might say this has always been the case.

What is more important is that this engagement with the enigmas of human existence is no less historical and ethical, as it grapples with "existential concerns over the traditional topics of myth, religion, and metaphysics that 'scientific' historiography rarely addresses" (White, 2005: 335). While this approach may offer a different aesthetic value compared to conventional academic historiographical texts, its aim is not necessarily beauty or sublimity, but rather to contemplate the people of the past with faith and humility (Doran, 2015). After all, for better or worse, they were no less human than us.

Curiosity, therefore, is paramount. Yet, in regions where geopolitics often unfolds through F-16s, rockets, and suicide bombers, it becomes indispensable. Thus, when historians act as the ultimate arbiters of right and wrong, they do not promote peaceful resolutions but rather add fuel to the fire. Perhaps, in the current moment, the ambivalent insights of "historical knowledge" are no longer pivotal for shaping a desired future. They might even be obstacles. However, even in such circumstances, it is crucial to acknowledge that no one owns the past. As Hayden White astutely noted, the past is something "all of us carry around with us in our daily lives and which we draw upon, willy-nilly and as best we can, for information, ideas, models, formulas, strategies, and the repressed memory, dreams, and desires of our lives" (White, 2014: 9).

Indeed, many of the original Zionists' dreams and desires were never fully realized, while others turned out to be nightmares. Nonetheless, if we dismiss these dreams with condescending lenses that only see elitist ideology, myth, and power, much of the historical essence of the movement disappears. As we briefly observed, for instance, in the case of Hebrew revival, overlooking the visceral intertwining of language and experience makes it difficult to explain the rapid transformation of Hebrew into a vernacular and a mother tongue.

This Element, therefore, suggests the potential for exploring the array of emotions and sensations evoked by Zionist dreams, envisioning a new Jewish lived experience as a pivotal element of the Zionist Revolution and modern Jewish life in Palestine. At least from a quantitative standpoint, this endeavor is not arduous or daunting, as Zionists often expressed their emotional and corporal aspirations. We might even argue that it constituted the primary theme of their writing. A few years prior to the establishment of the State of Israel in 1948, David Ben-Gurion, wrote:

> The meaning of the Jewish revolution is contained in one word, independence! Independence for the Jewish people in its homeland! Independence is not merely political or economic; it is also moral, cultural, and intellectual, and *it affects every limb and nerve of the body, every conscious and subconscious act*. Independence, too, means more than political and economic freedom; it involves also the spiritual, moral, and intellectual realms, and, in essence, *it is independence in the heart, in sentiment, and in will* (Hertzberg, 1997: 606, my emphasis).

For Ben-Gurion this radical change, which "affects every limb and nerve of the body," constitutes a "prolonged and continuing struggle" that will also involve future generations. Although much has changed since Ben-Gurion's words, the fears and confidence of "independence in the *heart*" are still very much present. Not limited to statehood, it is, a shared experience among "secular" Jewish Israelis from across the political spectrum. Even among many of the those who reside abroad and enjoy the diverse benefits of Western security and well-being.

This "different" experience in which Israelis set themselves apart from Jewish and non-Jewish counterparts in the West and the Middle East is manifested, for example, in the common use of the word *havaya* as an affirmative sign of deep feeling. This does not mean that the past and present overlap. In today's neoliberal world, the Israeli concept of *havaya* is often intertwined with consumption and enjoyment. For instance, a typical Israeli response to the question "how was the holiday in Greece?" might be "it was *havaya*" while a proper response to the question "how is the new wide-screen TV?" might be "it is *havaya*." Consequently, it is also common to hear a judge on the Israeli "imitations" of American Idol compliment a singer with the phrase like: "you took me through a *havaya*" (*He'evarta 'oti havaya*). Hence, despite the diverse and often consumerist contextualizations, many Israelis, like Gordon's original aspiration, understand experience as an emotional and non-linguistic moment of being there.

And yet, contemporary ideology and language cannot capture the historical *havaya* of the early twentieth-century. What does it mean, and feel, to revive one's body and soul? The few "strange Zionists" who embraced this radical endeavor have tried to tell us, but are we willing to listen? Let us hope, then, that future historians will remain open to the profound and sometimes unsettling words left by these often-radical men and women, as their legacy continues to surge forward, transforming the people of the past into us.

References

Alroey, Gur, 2004. *Jewish Immigration to the Land of Israel at the Early Twentieth Century* (Jerusalem: Yad-Ben-Zvi) [Hebrew].

Alroey, Gur, 2010. 'Review Pioneers: Passion or Zionists' Passion?' *Cathedra*, 137: 179–84.

Alroey, Gur, 2014. *An Unpromising Land: Jewish Migration to Palestine in the Early Twentieth Century* (Stanford, CA: Stanford University Press).

Alter, *Robert*, 1988. The *Invention of Hebrew Prose: Modern Fiction and the Language Revolution* (Seattle, WA: University of Washington Press).

Anderson, Amanda, Rita Felski, and Toril Moi, 2019. *Character: Three Inquiries in Literary Studies* (Chicago : Chicago University Press).

Appadurai, Arjun, 1996. *Modernity at Large: Cultural Dimensions of Globalization* (Minneapolis, MN: Minnesota University Press).

Avineri, Shalomo, 1981. *The Making of Modern Zionism: The Intellectual Origins of the Jewish State* (New York: Basic Books).

Barclay, Katie, 2020. *The History of Emotions: A Student Guide to Methods and Sources* (London: Red Globe Press).

Barclay, Katie, 2022. 'Compassion as an Agent of Historical Change,' *The American Historical Review*, 127 (4): 1752–85.

Bartal, Israel, 2005. *The Jews of Eastern Europe, 1772–1881* (Philadelphia, PA: Pennsylvania University Press).

Berdichevsky, Micha Josef, n.d. 'Divre Sifrut,' *Project Ben-Yehuda*, https://benyehuda.org/read/5562 [My translation, Hebrew].

Bialik, Hayim Nahman, 1950. 'Revealment and Concealment in Language,' (Trans. Jacob Sloan), *Commentary Magazine*, https://www.commentary.org/articles/hayim-bialik/cedars-of-lebanon-revealment-and-concealment-in-language/.

Boddice, Rob and Mark Smith, 2020. *Emotion, Sense, Experience* (Cambridge: Cambridge University Press).

Cohen, Roni and Olga Levitan, 2023. "Di Yidn Kumen!': Israeli and Multicultural Identities in Israeli Yiddish Light Entertainment Shows', *In geveb: A Journal of Yiddish Studies*, https://ingeveb.org/articles/israeli-yiddish-light-entertainment-shows.

Connerton, Paul, 2009. *How Societies Remember* (Cambridge: Cambridge University Press).

Darnton, Robert, 2009. *The Great Cat Massacre and Other Episodes in French Cultural History* (New York : Basic Books).

Dixon, Thomas, 2023. *The History of Emotions: A Very Short Introduction* (Oxford: Oxford University Press).

Doran, Robert, 2015. *The Theory of The Sublime from Longinus to Kant* (Cambridge: Cambridge University Press).

Doran, Robert, 2017. *The Ethics of Theory: Philosophy, History, Literature* (London: Bloomsbury).

Em Kol Hai, 1911a, May 26. 'Notes From my Travels to the Land of Israel,' *Hed ha-Zman* [Hebrew].

Em Kol Hai, 1911b, May 28. 'Notes From my Travels to the Land of Israel,' *Hed ha-Zman* [Hebrew].

Felski, Rita, 2020. *Hooked: Art and Attachment* (Chicago: University of Chicago Press).

Frankel, Jonathan, 1984. *Prophecy and Politics: Socialism, Nationalism and the Russian Jews, 1862–1917* (Cambridge: Cambridge University Press).

Fukuyama, Francis, 1992. *End of History and the Last Man* (New York: The Free Press).

Gold, Elon, 2023. 'Have You Ever Wondered Why Most Jews Don't Actually Speak Hebrew?,' *YouTube*, https://www.youtube.com/watch?v=66CRBhofQyM.

Gordon. Aharon David, 1912, December 6. 'Letter to Brenner,' *Hapoel Hatsair* [Hebrew].

Gordon. Aharon David, 2020. *Man and Nature*, eds. Yuval Jobani and Ron Margolin (Jerusalem: Magnes Press) [Hebrew].

Gumbrecht, Hans Ulrich, 2014. *Our Broad Present: Time and Contemporary Culture* (New York: Columbia University Press).

Halperin, Liora R., 2014. *Babel in Zion: Jews, Nationalism, and Language Diversity in Palestine, 1920–1948* (Yale, CT: Yale University Press).

Harshav, Benjamin, 1993. *Language in Time of Revolution* (Berkley, CA: University of California Press).

Helman, Anat, 2007. *Urban Culture in 1920s and 1930s Tel-Aviv*. Haifa: Haifa University Press. [Hebrew].

Helman, Anat, 2010. *Young Tel Aviv: A Tale of Two Cities* (Waltham, MA: Brandeis University Press).

Hertzberg, Arthur, 1997. *The Zionist Idea*: *A Historical Analysis and Reader* (Philadelphia, PA: The Jewish Publication Society).

Hobsbawm, Eric, 1995. *The Age of Extremes: The Short Twentieth Century, 1914–1991* (London: Abacus Books).

Idels, Ofer, 2022. 'How to Lose Gracefully in an Internationally Selfish World: Gender, The "New Jew" and the Underestimation of Athletic Performance in Interwar Palestine', *Journal of Modern Jewish Studies*, 21(2), 215–33.

Inbari, Assaf, 2000. 'Towards a Hebrew Literature,' *Azure*: 99–154. https://azure.org.il/download/magazine/165az9_inbari.pdf.

Kaplan, Eran, 2013. 'Post-Post-Zionism: A Paradigm Shift in Israel Studies?,' *Israel Studies Review*, 28(1): 142–55.

Kleinberg, Ethan, 2017. *Haunting History: For a Deconstructive Approach to the Past* (Stanford, CA: Stanford University Press).

Likhovsky, Asaf, 2010. 'Post-Post-Zionist Historiography,' *Israel Studies* 15(2): 1–23.

Moss, Kenneth B., 2009. *Jewish Renaissance in the Russian Revolution* (Cambridge, MA: Harvard University Press).

Moss, Kenneth B., 2021. *An Unchosen People: Jewish Political Reckoning in Interwar Poland*, (Cambridge, MA: Harvard University Press).

Neumann, Boaz, 2009. *Land and Desire in Early Zionism* (Tel Aviv: Am-Oved) [Hebrew].

Neumann, Boaz, 2011. *Land and Desire in Early Zionism* (Waltham, MA: Brandeis University Press).

Penslar, Derek, 2020. 'What's Love Got to Do with It? The Emotional Language of Early Zionism,' *Journal of Israeli History*, 38: 25–52.

Penslar, Derek, 2023. *Zionism: An Emotional State* (New Brunswick, NJ: Rutgers University Press).

Peretz, "Monish," 1888. The Yiddish Folk Library, The Steven Spielberg Digital Yiddish Library – 02379 [Yiddish].

Plamper, Jan, 2021. 'Sounds of February, Smells of October: The Russian Revolution as Sensory Experience,' *The American Historical Review*, 126(1): 140–65.

Rabinowitz to Ruppin, 1914, Central Zionist Archive, L2-135–1 [Hebrew].

Razi, Tammy, 2011. 'Review of Young Tel Aviv: A Tale of Two Cities,' *Journal of Israeli History*, 30(2): 240–42.

Reddy, William M., 2001. *The Navigation of Feeling: A Framework for the History of Emotions* (Cambridge: Cambridge University Press).

Reddy, William M., 2020. 'The Unavoidable Intentionality of Affect: The History of Emotions and the Neurosciences of the Present Day,' *Emotion Review*, 12(3): 168–78.

Ricoeur, Paul, 1970. *Freud and Philosophy an Essay on Interpretation* (New Haven, CT: Yale University Press).

Rojanski, Rachel, 2020. *Yiddish in Israel: A History* (Bloomington, IN: Indiana University Press).

Rosenwein, Barbara H., 2002. 'Worrying about Emotions in History,' *The American Historical Review*, 107(3): 821–45.

Runia, Eelco, 2014. *Moved by the Past: Discontinuity and Historical Mutation* (New York: Columbia University Press).

Saposnik, Arieh, 2008. *Becoming Hebrew: The Creation of a Jewish National Culture in Ottoman Palestine* (Oxford: Oxford University Press).

Scott, Joan W. 1991. 'The Evidence of Experience,' *Critical Inquiry*, 17 (4): 773–97.

Shapira, Anita, 2012. *Israel: A History* (Waltham, MA: Brandeis University Press).

Shavit, Zohar, 2004, July 4. 'Review of Jewish Immigration to Palestine in the Early Twentieth Century, *Ha'aretz* [Hebrew].

Shavit, Zohar, 2017. 'Can It Be That Our Dormant Language Has Been Wholly Revived?': Vision, Propaganda, and Linguistic Reality in the Yishuv Under the British Mandate,' *Israel Studies*, 22(1): 101–38.

Shoham, Hizky, 2013. 'Review of Young Tel Aviv: A Tale of Two Cities,' *AJS Review*, 37(2): 432.

Vital, David, 1980. *The Origins of Zionism* (Oxford: Oxford University Press).

Wallach, Yair, 2020. *A City in Fragments: Urban Text in Modern Jerusalem* (Stanford, CA: Stanford University Press).

White, Hayden, 1973. *Metahistory: The Historical Imagination in Nineteenth-century Europe* (Baltimore, MD: Johns Hopkins University Press).

White, Hayden, 2005. 'The Public Relevance of Historical Studies: A Reply to Dirk Moses,' *History and Theory*, 44(3): 333–8.

White, Hayden, 2014. The Practical Past (Evanston: Northwestern University Press).

Wrobel, Magdalena, 2018. 'Review of An Unpromising Land: Jewish Migration to Palestine in the Early Twentieth Century', *East European Jewish Affairs*, 48(2–3): 322–4.

Zahra, Tara, 2016. *The Great Departure: Mass Migration from Eastern Europe and the Making of the Free World* (New York: W.W. Norton).

Žižek, Slaovj, 1994. 'Introduction: The Spectre of Ideology', in Slaovj Žižek (ed.), *Mapping Ideology* (New York: Verso).

Zuckermann, Ghil'ad, 2008. *Israeli – A Beautiful Language* (Tel Aviv: Am Oved).

Acknowledgments

I would like to extend my gratitude to the editors of the Elements on Histories of Emotions and the Senses series, Rob Boddice, Piroska Nagy, and Mark Smith, for their interest in this Element. The core ideas of the project were presented at the HEX Seminar and annual conference at Tampere University, the Colloquium of the Center for the History of Emotions at the Max Planck Institute in Berlin, the Biennial Conference of the Society of the History of Emotions in Florence, the Sound, Language & the Making of Urban Space conference at the University of Copenhagen, and The North American Chapter on the History of Emotion in Vancouver. I am thankful to all the listeners for their questions, which significantly improved this Element. My dear friend Roni Cohen provided valuable remarks for section 3 and served as a constant source of knowledge, encouragement, and support. I also remain grateful to the Humboldt Foundation and Minerva Foundation for granting me the valuable time to think and write this project. Last but not least, I want to express my appreciation to my family, especially my daughters Amalia and Yael, for providing me with all the emotions from A to Y.

Cambridge Elements ≡

Histories of Emotions and the Senses

Series Editors

Rob Boddice
Tampere University

Rob Boddice (PhD, FRHistS) is Senior Research Fellow at the Academy of Finland Centre of Excellence in the History of Experiences. He is the author/editor of thirteen books, including *Knowing Pain: A History of Sensation, Emotion and Experience* (Polity Press, 2023), *Humane Professions: The Defence of Experimental Medicine, 1876–1914* (Cambridge University Press, 2021) and A History of Feelings (Reaktion, 2019).

Piroska Nagy
Université du Québec à Montréal (UQAM)

Piroska Nagy is Professor of Medieval History at the Université du Québec à Montréal (UQAM) and initiated the first research program in French on the history of emotions. She is the author or editor of fourteen volumes, including *Le Don des larmes au Moyen Âge* (Albin Michel, 2000); *Medieval Sensibilities: A History of Emotions in the Middle Ages*, with *Damien Boquet* (Polity, 2018); and *Histoire des émotions collectives: Épistémologie, émergences*, expériences, with D. Boquet and L. Zanetti Domingues (Classiques Garnier, 2022).

Mark Smith
University of South Carolina

Mark Smith (PhD, FRHistS) is Carolina Distinguished Professor of History and Director of the Institute for Southern Studies at the University of South Carolina. He is author or editor of over a dozen books and his work has been translated into Chinese, Korean, Danish, German, and Spanish. He has lectured in Europe, throughout the United States, Australia, and China and his work has been featured in the New York Times, the London Times, the Washington Post, and the Wall Street Journal. He serves on the US Commission for Civil Rights.

About the Series

Born of the emotional and sensory "turns", Elements in Histories of Emotions and the Senses move one of the fastest-growing interdisciplinary fields forward. The series is aimed at scholars across the humanities, social sciences, and life sciences, embracing insights from a diverse range of disciplines, from neuroscience to art history and economics. Chronologically and regionally broad, encompassing global, transnational, and deep history, it concerns such topics as affect theory, intersensoriality, embodiment, human-animal relations, and distributed cognition. The founding editor of the series was Jan Plamper.

Cambridge Elements ≡

Histories of Emotions and the Senses

Elements in the Series

Feeling Terrified?: The Emotions of Online Violent Extremism
Lise Waldek, Julian Droogan and Catharine Lumby

Making Noise in the Modern Hospital
Victoria Bates

Academic Emotions: Feeling the Institution
Katie Barclay

*Sensory Perception, History and Geology: The Afterlife of Molyneux's Question
in British, American and Australian Landscape Painting and Cultural Thought*
Richard Read

Love in Contemporary Technoculture
Ania Malinowska

Memes, History and Emotional Life
Katie Barclay and Leanne Downing

Boredom
Elena Carrera

*Marketing Violence: The Affective Economy of Violent Imageries
in the Dutch Republic*
Frans-Willem Korsten, Inger Leemans, Cornelis van der Haven
and Karel Vanhaesebrouck

Beyond Compassion: Gender and Humanitarian Action
Dolores Martín-Moruno

Uncertainty and Emotion in the 1900 Sydney Plague
Philippa Nicole Barr

*Sensorium: Contextualizing the Senses and Cognition in History
and Across Cultures*
David Howes

Zionism: Emotions, Language and Experience
Ofer Idels

A full series listing is available at: www.cambridge.org/EHES

Printed in the United States
by Baker & Taylor Publisher Services